FODOR'S

FUN IN

NEW YORK CITY

1988

FODOR'S TRAVEL PUBLICATIONS, INC.
New York & London

ISBN 0–679–01511–6
ISBN 0–340–41964–4   (Hodder & Stoughton)

Maps and plans by Pictograph
Illustrations by Ted Burwell

New titles in the series

Barbados
Jamaica

also available

Acapulco
Bahamas
Disney World & the Orlando Area
Las Vegas
London
Maui
Montreal
New Orleans
Paris
Rio
St. Martin/St. Maarten
San Francisco
Waikiki

Contents

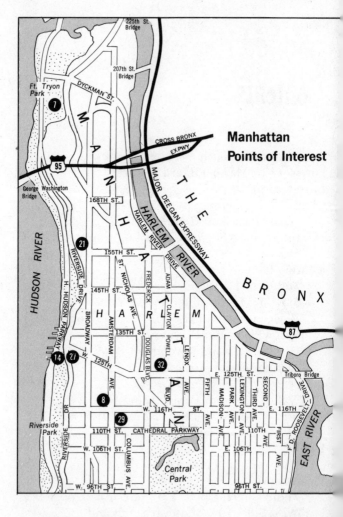

**Manhattan
Points of Interest**

Points of Interest

1) American Museum of Natural History
2) Carnegie Hall
3) Central Park Zoo
4) Chinatown
5) Citicorp Center
6) City Hall
7) Cloisters
8) Columbia University
9) Empire State Building
10) Frick Museum
11) Gracie Mansion
12) Gramercy Park
13) Grand Central Station
14) Grant's Tomb
15) Guggenheim Museum
16) Hayden Planetarium
17) Jacob J. Javits Convention Center
18) Lincoln Center
19) Madison Square Garden
20) Metropolitan Museum of Art

Foreword

By Mayor Edward I. Koch

Of all the wonders of New York, the greatest is its status as an open city. It has no boundaries, no frontiers, no lines of demarcation. So you want to be a New Yorker? Consider yourself one and you are one.

Because New York is a city-state of mind, its possibilities are infinite. Creativity, in the arts, in business, in virtually every field of human endeavor, flows from this openness. Nothing surprises us here. Everything changes. Some people have pictured New York as harsh and callous. Not true. It is clear-eyed and tolerant.

The bigness and busyness of all the world's diversity compressed in one place can be unnerving. There are even natives who venture into unfamiliar precincts with a sense of trepidation. This is a shame, and an unnecessary shame. New York is meant to awaken the sense of adventure in every heart.

Take art. No visitor should miss the encyclopedic marvels of the Metropolitian Museum of Art and the breathtaking pleasures of the Museum of Modern Art (MOMA to you and me). But is there a better way to feel at home with the beauty of great art than getting to know the mansion that houses the Frick Collection? And what about the exotic rewards of the sumptuous collection of Tibetan art found in a modest house and garden on Staten Island?

Take music. Of course, there is the grandest of grand opera. And a dizzying array of orchestras and groups and performers. But there is also the most modern of modern jazz in this club or that. There are cocktail lounge smoothies. There is a revivified folk music scene in Greenwich Village. There are punks and performance artists and piccolo players. As Leonard Cohen wrote, "There is music on Clinton Street . . ." and, it seems, on every street.

Take theater. Every time somebody starts to write "Broadway is dead," it comes alive with a burst of innovation and high-energy entertainment. But in New York, theater also means revisionist Shakespeare Off-Broadway, the unknown playwright experimenting Off-Off-Broadway, a new combination of music and dance and words and sounds and movement and backdrops in a Soho loft.

In New York, a painter can experience the frenzy of the New York Stock Exchange trading floor from the viewing gallery. A stockbroker can learn to sculpt at the Art Students League. Both — and everyone else — can stalk birds in the marshlands of the Jamaica Bay Wildlife Refuge in Queens.

Use this guidebook to pick up the trails and open the doors. And then use your senses to discover the rest. Walk streets that are unlike any other streets in the world. Absorb the energy.

Visit George Washington's pew at St. Paul's Chapel and reflect on New York's role as the nation's first capital. Admire the Statue of Liberty, but don't forget Ellis Island, gateway to the future for most of our forebears. Gaze on the mighty Palisades of the Hudson River from the bluffs of Riverdale in the Bronx. Savor harbor and skyline from the Brooklyn Heights Promenade. Is there a greater urban view anywhere?

There is too much to do and too much to take in. It is a life's work. That's why there's no such thing as staying too long in New York. You simply move faster, talk quickly and speed up your way of thinking.

It may seem daunting at first, but remember the saving grace: Wherever you come from, you are home in New York.

Introduction

By Kathleen Beckett

If you are looking for fun, this is the place: Fun City. New York earns its nickname; it serves up amusements that are not only the most varied but also the best in the world. From ballgames to ballets, rock concerts to symphony orchestras, street art to museum exhibits, walks in the park to walks on the wild side (sometimes one and the same thing), New York has it all, unsurpassed in range, quality, and excitement—and it has it nonstop, 24 hours a day.

The fun can, admittedly, cost a small fortune. New York has been rated the most expensive city for restaurants—as well as hotels—in the country. A night on the town, complete with dinner at a top restaurant, tickets to a Broadway show, entrance to a nightclub, a few drinks and a cab ride home could require mortgaging the home to foot the bill.

On the other hand, one of the qualities that makes New York so vibrant is the range of its entertainments, including those that come absolutely free. Window-shopping, people-watching, gallery-hopping, skyscraper-gaping, celebrity-scouting, and, especially in the sum-

mer, a full schedule of free concerts and plays won't set
you back one penny.

And there are myriad midcost activities that will ex-
pose you to the experimental creativity—in all the arts—
that is a New York City hallmark: Off- and Off-Off-Broadway plays, jazz clubs, coffeehouses, loft recitals, poetry
readings, film festivals, museum shows, and up-and-coming restaurants provide inexpensive showcases for the
wealth of raw energy and talent that resides in Manhattan's few square miles.

New Yorkers are a rare breed, willing to forego crea-
ture comforts such as backyards, and in some cases hot
running water, for the chance to live out both private
dreams and the great American dream. Your cab driver
could be the next best-selling author; your waitress, the
toast of Broadway. Their zest, resourcefulness, mettle,
drive, and spirit are infectious.

Simply walking down the streets of the city, you can
feel a sense of expectation and possibility. The action—
that proverbial hustle and bustle—goes on around the
clock. The pace gets in your blood after a block or two:
your step quickens as you are carried along by the flow
of taxis and the streams of pedestrians, always, it seems,
with someplace pressing to go.

New York's architecture can inspire awe, from the
soaring spires of its skyscrapers to the subtler delights of
an intricate wrought iron railing welcoming you up the
steps of a graceful old town house.

The city's neighborhoods echo the diversity. Within
walking distance you can voyage from the pagoda telephone booths of Chinatown to the espresso bars of Little
Italy to the former warehouses of Soho that now enjoy a
new lease on life as artists' lofts and galleries. A mere
subway ride separates the proud old apartment buildings
lining Park Avenue—emblems of established wealth and
conservatism—from the sometimes raunchy but consistently adventurous potpourri of boutiques, eateries,
clubs, galleries, street life, and tenement living in the
East Village.

With all this splendid diversity to discover, how un-
fortunate that many visitors with little time to explore
head straight to Times Square, noted for its theaters and

New Year's Eve celebrations, but now characterized
more by X-rated movie houses and massage parlors.
These visitors wonder how anyone can live in New York.
New Yorkers, passing through Times Square, wonder
the same thing, and most residents avoid the area unless
they have theater tickets.

The best place really to capture the city's spirit is the
Grand Army Plaza, at the southeast corner of Central
Park. Here is the heart of New York in all its splendor;
here is New York at your feet. The skyscrapers of Central
Park South and West border the park in looming preci-
sion, visible through the trees, their lights twinkling in
the night. Fifth Avenue, with its parade of buses, limos,
and yellow taxis, sweeps by on its long and broad
progression from nearly one end of town to the other.
The city's finest hotels—the Plaza, the Pierre, the Sherry
Netherland—are clustered here, as are, within blocks,
the premiere shops. And you are at the entrance to the
city's happiest and most extensive piece of real estate,
Central Park.

It is said that Central Park helps many New Yorkers
retain their sanity. A stroll along its leafy, winding paths
can be as restorative as a weekend in the country. If you
like horseback riding, jogging, bicycling, sunbathing,
picnicking, cross-country skiing, bocci, ice-skating, zoos,
Shakespeare in the Park, and opera and symphony concerts (the yearly *1812 Overture* ends in an explosion of
fireworks over the city's skyline), you'll find it here. Call
the New York City Parks Department (360–8111) for
information.

Bordering the park to the east is New York's famed
Upper East Side, perhaps the most affluent bedroom and
playground in the world. The blocks off Fifth Avenue are
lined with impressive limestone mansions and gracious
brownstones. Madison Avenue houses the world's top
designer boutiques (Yves Saint Laurent, Ungaro, Gi-
venchy), art galleries, and antique shops. Lexington Avenue boasts Bloomingdale's, and First Avenue the
much-talked-about uptown bar scene —watering holes
such as Adam's Apple and Maxwell's Plum. Back on Fifth
Avenue is Museum Mile, starting at 103rd Street with the
Museum of the City of New York and descending to the

International Center of Photography at 94th Street, the mixing bowl Guggenheim Museum at 88th Street, the Whitney Museum of American Art over on Madison Avenue at 74th Street, and the mammoth Metropolitan Museum of Art, on the park side of Fifth at 82nd Street.

Across the park is the trendy Upper West Side. Long a neighborhood of families, intellectuals, immigrants, Columbia University students, and theater folk, it is now the scene of some controversy, as hot new restaurants, shops, and cafes nose out less showy, more mainstream establishments. The scene along Columbus Avenue is certainly worth a visit to check out the cutting edge of style, cuisine, and the art of seeing and being seen. And it is a good place to grab a bite to eat before heading to the West Side's cultural emporium, Lincoln Center, with its opera, ballet, and symphony halls.

South of Central Park from 59th Street to 34th Street, river to river, is Midtown, with its skyscrapers, department stores, great hotels, legendary restaurants and a plethora of coffeeshops, Rockefeller Center, the United Nations, St. Patrick's Cathedral, Fashion Avenue (another name for Seventh Avenue south of 42nd Street), the Empire State Building—in short, many of the places that are symbols of the city.

South of 34th Street to 14th Street, the city changes textures. This is the location of many manufacturing shops and small businesses of New York, and the neighborhood tends to "close up" at 5 P.M. Two residential pockets are worth visits. Gramercy Park, at 21st Street off Third Avenue, is reminiscent of the quiet beauty of a London square with its historic townhouses and private patch of green. And Chelsea, in the 20s west of Seventh Avenue, combines a fascinating mix of history (the Chelsea Hotel—home to famous and infamous iconoclasts from Mark Twain to Sid Vicious as well as the lovely old brownstone where *The Night Before Christmas* was written) and the very latest in shops and restaurants.

Between 14th Street and Houston Street (pronounced "How-ston" here), lies Greenwich Village. Washington Square Park, with its arch (reminiscent of the *Arc de Triomphe* in Paris), is the epicenter, surrounded by the quiet tree-lined streets, New York University students, coffeehouses, boutiques, bookstores, and bistros that have turned the Village into a legend. The West Village holds the more traditional pleasures—blocks of beautiful old buildings and brick sidewalks, made for meandering; shops full of antiques and all kinds of artistic expression, from clothing to canvases—and the center of the gay community on Christopher Street. The East Village, centered on St. Mark's Place, is where punk still lives, where Sam Shepard wrote his first plays, Patty Smith and the Ramones first shook things up at CBGB & OMFUGS, where Keith Haring and Jean-Michel Basquiat got their starts as artists. The artistic creativity here is so explosive that those who can't wait for a gallery show have painted the very sidewalks under your feet.

South of Houston Street, Soho, with all its art galleries, is quite the place to be on weekends. Many artists turned the area's warehouses into residential lofts until higher and higher rents—and the doctors and lawyers who could afford them—drove many to Tribeca, just to the south. As things work in New York, the trendiest little shops and galleries and restaurants and clubs have followed, making Tribeca one of the city's more interesting neighborhoods to head to in the evening. Nearby are some of the city's best-known ethnic enclaves—China-town, Little Italy, and the Lower East Side, with its delis and Sunday discount shopping—and the South Street Seaport district, the looming towers of the World Trade Center, and Wall Street, where a visit to the New York Stock Exchange will give new meaning to the word "frantic."

Off the tip of Manhattan stands the Statue of Liberty, resplendent after her 100th birthday with a new facelift.

To get your bearings, head to the New York Convention and Visitors Bureau at Columbus Circle (the junction of 59th Street and Central Park West) for information on sightseeing tours, the city's bus and subway system, hotels, motels, and restaurants, as well as seasonal listings of entertainment events. (See *General Information* chapter.)

A terrific way to see the city in all its glory is by sailing completely around it. The Circle Line encircles Manhattan, weaving under bridges, past the Statue of

Liberty, alongside the remarkable skyline. Even the most jaded New Yorkers find the trip a thrill. (See *Touring the City* chapter below.)

For information on events in the city, there are a number of good sources to reach for. *New York* magazine, a weekly publication, has complete listings of cultural events, shopping, sports, street fairs, walking tours, museums and galleries, children's activities, and special events. The magazine also provides a free ticket service, Monday through Friday from 12:30 P.M. to 6:30 P.M., 880–1755, providing information about the availability of tickets for theater, dance, and concerts.

The venerable weekly *New Yorker* magazine also contains listings, with a bit of commentary, for the theater, dance, nightlife, jazz/folk/rock concerts, art galleries, museums and libraries, music, sports, and movies. And the *New York Times'* special "Weekend" section on Friday and "Arts & Leisure" and "Guide" sections on Sundays are good to consult for upcoming events. For more offbeat listings—rock concerts, performance art, loft recitals—the *Village Voice,* hitting the newsstands on Wednesdays, is a good bet.

General Information

There is no best or worst time to visit New York City. The metropolis is truly a year-round city. But spring and autumn are especially glorious. Hotels' busiest times are September through November.

Depending on your own interests, consider a number of annual seasonal happenings. In winter, the indoor boat or antique shows are a big draw; for opera fans, the Met's season is from mid-September to early May. Summer can be dreadfully hot and humid, but it is an ongoing festival of free concerts, plays, and exhibits. And sports fans can root for the Yankees or Mets in the summer, the Giants or Jets in the fall, or the Rangers in winter. December draws a big crowd to the Big Apple to see the city festooned for the holidays. Word of warning: **Do not** attempt to drive to New York if you can help it at any time of the year, but especially during the holiday season. Traffic is heavily congested and nerves and tempers are frayed. Enjoy the city on foot. You'll see more, too.

WHAT TO PACK

New York City is in the temperate zone, but weather can jump to extremes. Summer temperatures, officially, rarely go above 90 degrees, but when they do, and the humidity matches the heat, sundresses and open sandals for women and the lightest weight slacks for men are the only route to go for sightseeing. Shorts usually are for the beach, boating, or weekend sunning and picnicking in Central Park. Running and jogging suits are also for those activities during the week and maybe for a casual brunch on weekends.

Hotels, restaurants, and stores are well air-conditioned in summer and sometimes overheated in winter. So the layered look is practical for New York dressing. A smart raincoat with a zip-in lining is invaluable. Heavy snows are a rarity in New York, but blizzards, even in early spring, are not unknown. When a few inches of snow does fall, the heat from the sidewalks' underground pipes and tunnels melts the flakes quickly.

But whatever the season, comfortable shoes are a must for enjoying the city. New Yorkers are great walkers.

In general, New York is a fashion-conscious city. The casual but "put-together-with-style" look is acceptable in most restaurants, theaters, hotels, and the new nightclubs. Designer jeans are worn widely. The relaxed look holds—except for some deluxe restaurants, where jackets and ties are expected for men, and women will want to show off a stunning outfit. When making dinner reservations, ask what dress is required.

GETTING THERE

Of the three airports serving New York, John F. Kennedy is the largest and serves most of the international traffic. JFK is also the most difficult to get in and out of, so worth avoiding, if possible. Most domestic airlines serve both LaGuardia and Newark airports, too. LaGuardia is the smallest of the three airports and only 30 minutes from midtown Manhattan. Newark is across the Hudson River, in New Jersey. It's about 50 minutes from Midtown. Express bus and taxi services are available at all three airports.

Carey Transportation's buses (718–632–0500) run frequently from Kennedy and LaGuardia to Midtown. The Carey buses deposit passengers rather unceremoniously at Park Avenue off 42nd Street, right across from Grand Central Terminal, or at one of three midtown hotels—Marriott Marquis, Times Square; New York Hilton, Rockefeller Center; and Sheraton City Squire, 700 Seventh Ave. For those making connections to Newark Airport, however, buses continue on to the Port Authority Bus Terminal on the West Side, at Eighth Ave. and 42nd St. There, passengers board New Jersey Transit (201–762–5100 or 800–772–2222 in New Jersey) buses, which run frequently between Newark and the bus terminal. One-way fares are $8 from JFK, $6 from LaGuardia, and $5 from Newark.

On arrival at any of the airports, expect to find cab lines at the taxi stalls. Fares are about $25 from JFK and $15 from LaGuardia, including tip. Tolls for bridges and tunnels are extra. If you get on line to share a cab with fellow travelers you can save some money. To compute the fare from Newark, add an extra $10 to the meter reading to account for the cab's return trip. Total should be about $35.

Be on guard for the entrepreneurial-type cab drivers, some of whom prey on unsuspecting visitors and try to overcharge. One of the tricks is to suggest that the passenger share a ride with others. The cabbie then tries to collect the total fare from each of the riders. That's illegal and should be reported to the city's Taxi Complaints Bureau, 869–4237.

New York City's two major train terminals are Pennsylvania Station, at Seventh Ave. and 32nd St., and Grand Central Terminal, Park Ave. and 42nd St. (Grand Central is a National Landmark building, now in the final stages of a total refurbishment.) Incoming trains, depending on their route, arrive at one or the other station, but never stop at both. Buses arrive at the Port Authority Bus Terminal, Eighth Ave. and 42nd St.

At each terminal, taxis can be hailed on the street outside; subways and buses are close by (see *Getting Around* section below). A word of caution about taking a cab from these points: Be careful of street men who offer to hail a cab for you and expect payment. Better to ignore them and try to hail one yourself.

Arriving at the Big Apple in style? Arrange for a *London Towncar* limo to meet you (988–9700). Be prepared to pay about $70 for the service from JFK or Newark and $60 from LaGuardia.

We strongly discourage driving into New York City because of limited parking facilities and congestion. If drive you must, however, there are car rental agencies at airline terminals and throughout the city. These include *Avis* (800–331–1212), *Hertz* (800–654–3131), and *National* (800–328–4567).

There are various combinations of bridges, tunnels, and expressways that funnel automobile traffic into Manhattan. From west and south, Highways I–78, I–80, and I–95 take you to the city by the Lincoln Tunnel, Holland Tunnel, or the George Washington Bridge. From the north, the New York State Thruway, I–87, or the New England Thruway, I–95, leads to New York. The FDR Drive is the main artery for traffic to travel north and south. It parallels the East River. You'll pay a toll ($3) when crossing the Hudson River and entering New York City, but not when leaving. Consult your local automobile club for suggestions on the best route to take from your place of departure.

When parking in New York City, remember to keep a close watch on the parking rules. The fee for reclaiming a car that has been towed away in violation of the rules is a hefty $100 in cash—in addition to the parking fine.

INFORMATION SERVICES

Free visitors information: The *New York Convention and Visitors Bureau*, 2 Columbus Circle (397–8222), or its *Times Square Information* booth at 158 West 42nd St. (no phone). The unbiased organization is a font of information on anything that involves the Big Apple. Visits are encouraged. They are open 9 A.M.–6 P.M. Monday through Friday, and 10 A.M.–6 P.M. weekends and holidays.

Useful numbers: The area code for Manhattan and the Bronx is 212. Brooklyn, Queens, and Staten Island were given their own area code, 718. Although interdialing between these two area codes may seem like calling long distance, there is no extra charge for such calls. The charge for calling throughout the city from a pay station is 25 cents.

For any emergency help—ambulance, fire, or police—dial 911. Other numbers that may be useful: free daily events, 360–1333; international calls, dial 0 for operator; local directory assistance, 411; long distance calls, 1, plus area code, plus number; long distance information, 1, plus area code, plus 555–1212; time, 976–1616; travel information, 397–8222; 24-hour pharmacy, 755–2266; weather, 976–1212.

GETTING AROUND

To really see and savor New York, your best bet is to do each section—Midtown, Wall Street, Greenwich Village, Soho, Tribeca, etc.—on foot. But when public transportation is needed, or when your feet have cried "Stop," you'll find New York has an extensive network of buses, subways, and taxis.

Midtown Manhattan is laid out in a grid, which makes it easy to get one's bearings. Avenues run north and south, with Fifth Avenue the dividing line between

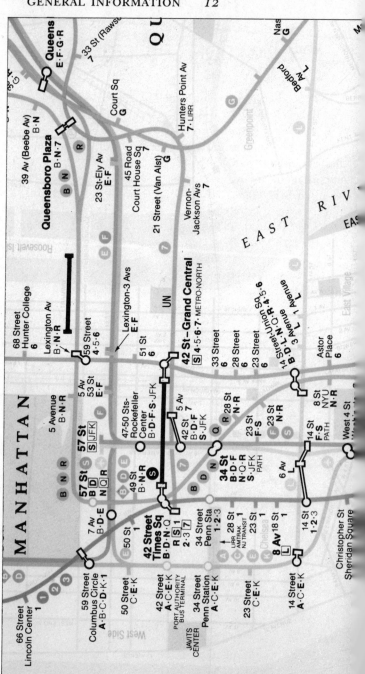

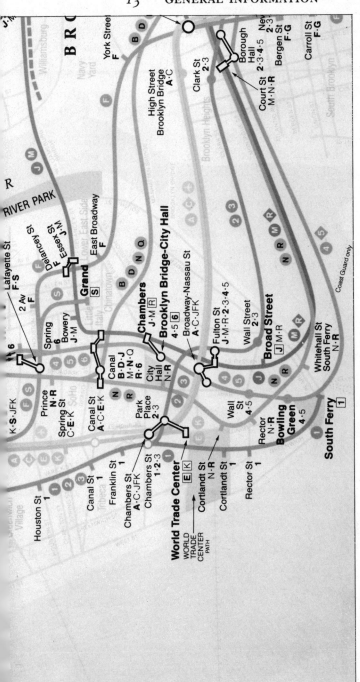

the east and west sides of town. Streets run east and west, with the traffic generally flowing east on the even-numbered streets and west on the odd-numbered. Crosstown blocks along the streets (between avenues) are generally long; avenue blocks are a half to a third that distance—so a 20- or 30-block stroll along an avenue is not an especially long walk.

Broadway, the longest street in the world, meanders diagonally down the length of Manhattan. In Greenwich Village and Lower Manhattan (Wall Street area, the oldest part of the city) the streets are less logically laid out than in Midtown.

Get the lay of the land by studying a subway map. On the preceding two pages is a map of the Midtown and Lower Manhattan areas. Complete maps are available free at token booths at Grand Central, Penn Station, or Jay Street, Brooklyn, where Transit Authority offices are located. Or pick up the *I Love NY Travel Guide* from the New York Convention and Visitors Bureau. You can call the bureau's Information Center at 397–8222 to get exact instructions on the best way to get from Point A to Point B from anywhere in the city. (Subway information also is supplied by calling the Transit Authority at 718–330–1234, but be prepared for a long wait.)

The subway is still the fastest way to get around New York. Study your map and join some of the 3.5 million riders who use the 230 miles of subway lines each weekday. For comfort's sake, avoid the subway during rush hours (7:30–9 A.M. and 4:30–6 P.M.). And for safety's sake, avoid the subways late at night. If you must use them then, choose a car in the middle of the train, where the conductor and most riders are. A subway token, purchased at any subway station, costs $1 as of this writing.

New York's **bus** system, with its 1,000 miles of routes, while slower than the subway, affords you a better chance to sightsee and people-watch. Since most buses stop every other block, they usually will land you closer to your destination than the subway. Fare is also $1 in exact change or subway token. Transfers are issued free upon the request of the passenger. They allow you to make one continuing trip on a number of bus routes, generally perpendicular to your original route. The acceptable transfer routes are listed on the back of the transfer slip. Don't forget to ask the driver for one when you board your bus.

There are some 12,000 licensed **taxis** in New York. Based on cab fares in other cities, New York costs are considered reasonable. The meter drop for the first tenth of a mile is $1.15 plus 15¢ for each additional ninth of a mile. A 15 to 20 percent tip is the norm. To hail a cab— vacant cabs have a number lit up on the roof—a wave of the hand from sidewalk's edge will do. But be prepared to be ignored at times, particularly when it's raining.

When possible, automobiles should be left at home. Parking is at a premium, unless you don't mind shelling out $20 a night to park in the Midtown area.

For a special evening on the town, go like the millionaires and hire a chauffeur-driven **limousine.** *Carey Cadillac* charges $25 an hour; *Fugazy Continental,* which carries six passengers and has stereo and TVs, goes for $26 an hour.

Touring the City

By Melanie Menagh

Seeing the sights is the reason many of New York City's 17 million annual visitors come to the Big Apple. The best way to see those sights—both human and man-made —is by taking walking tours of various neighborhoods, as described in detail below.

For a get-acquainted overview of the city, however, we suggest the walking tour be preceded by an organized sightseeing tour. Hundreds of different combinations of these, both riding and afoot, are available. Among them are *Grayline* (397–2600) and *Manhattan Sightseeing* (869–5005), which offer bus tours from a quickie 2½-hour look ($12.50) to a comprehensive tour of 8½ hours ($28.50), which will take you uptown, downtown, and then some.

A totally different perspective of New York's fabulous skyline can be gained on a three-hour narrated boat ride around the isle of Manhattan on the *Circle Line* (563–3200). Boats operate from a pier on the Hudson River at the western end of 42nd Street, April to mid-November, at a bargain $12. On the more elegant side, you can view the Midtown and Lower Manhattan skylines while dining on a mouth-watering buffet aboard the luxurious *River-anda* or *Empress of New York* yacht. (See *Lower Midtown*

section below.) A splendid view of the Lower Manhattan
skyline—and the Statue of Liberty as well—can be enjoyed aboard the *Staten Island Ferry* for only 25¢ round-
trip.

There's probably no more refreshing way to see the
Lower Manhattan skyline than aboard one of the four
sailing vessels that ply the waters during summer months
from the South Street Seaport and Battery Park. The
Pioneer, Petrel, Francy, and *Ventura* offer majestic views of
the towers and the Statue of Liberty. Newest to the fleet
is the sturdy, red-and-white side-wheeler, the *Andrew
Fletcher.* Cruises range in price from $5 to $15.

For a thrilling—and literal—overview of the city, call
Island Helicopter (683–4575).

Getting back down to earth, we're now ready to start
our walking tours of the Big Apple. What follows is a
description of a few selective sights you may expect to
find in each of the neighborhoods. Of course, you may
want to be more adventuresome and explore more than
we offer. By all means, do so. That's part of the fun of
seeing New York City.

MIDTOWN

Midtown embodies everybody's vision of New York
City: sky-high buildings, sidewalks choked with people in
a hurry. Here are the department stores, theaters, and
restaurants with the greatest clout and cachet in America.
If you were a dress you'd want to debut on Fifth Avenue;
if you were a dress rehearsal you'd want to debut on West
45th Street; if you were dressed duck you'd want to debut
on a Midtown table. All of the things for which Manhattan is famous—and infamous—can be found from river
to river between 42nd Street and Central Park.

New Yorkers have a love/hate relationship with Midtown. For some New Yorkers, the urban cityscape here—
the convergence of culture, couture, and cuisine—is
their chief excuse for the superiority they feel over mere
mortals whose cities are sadly some other place. For

other New Yorkers, here is a place out of which they must get as soon after 5 P.M. as possible.

You can begin your tour by taking a swan dive into the middle of the madness: Times Square. They've torn it down and slapped up a new one, and are threatening to redo it all over again, but the ruling powers of the place seem determined that harmony will never be at home here, anarchy will prevail, assaulting your sensory circuits with a constant barrage of color and noise and movement.

Although the anarchy is most obvious at night when the bright lights are working in earnest, there are lots of sights to be sampled during the day. If you're hankering to see a show, you may want to wait in the **TKTS** line, at 47th Street and Broadway or at No. 2 World Trade Center, for half-price tickets, which are available to all but the very hottest shows. If you have your heart set on seeing the season's box-office blockbuster, but didn't call months in advance, you can try to get standing room tickets sold at most theaters on the day of performance, or inquire if there have been any returns for the evening's performance.

And if you can't get enough theater from your seat, drop by 228 West 47th St., where you can pick up a tour at **Backstage on Broadway,** which will take you exactly there. Still not satisfied? Then satiate your thespian appetites with a visit to the **Theatre Museum,** 1515 Broadway, in the tunnel between 44th and 45th streets, where you'll enjoy a feast of costumes, recordings, and playbills from Shakespeare to Sondheim.

Proceed from Times Square down to 42nd Street. To your right (west) is Theater Row, between 9th and 10th avenues, and on the river is the **Circle Line,** which offers a circumnavigation of Manhattan.

To the left (east), the green you see peeking out across Sixth Avenue is Bryant Park. At the rear of the famous "Lion Library," the park has one of the lushest lawns in Manhattan, and in summertime the young professionals deploy themselves thereupon, imbibing liberal doses of sun, tofutti, and live jazz that is presented most days around lunchtime.

Music lovers will also want to stop in at the booth on the 42nd Street side of the park to pick up some half-price tickets for any music or dance performance—from the opera or the Philharmonic to the Alvin Ailey dancers or Phillip Glass.

The main branch of the **Public Library** has had New Yorkers reading between the lions since it was erected by Carière and Hastings in 1911 on the site of a former potters field. Even if you're not heavy into research, the library's interior is as bountifully beaux arts as its exterior, and hosts exhibitions on subjects ranging from archaeology to zoology.

If you can plow your way through the crowds crisscrossing Fifth Avenue, do pause occasionally for an upward glance at the Chrysler Building, New Yorkers' uncontested favorite, glistening against a blue sky, as you continue eastward to the **Whitney Museum of Art at Phillip Morris** (120 Park Ave.). You can sip espresso in the sculpture garden and enjoy **Grand Central's** famous face through the several-story windows.

Keeping an eye on everyone's comings and goings are Mercury, Hercules, and Minerva, perched precariously above the 13-foot clock. If you want to know all there is to know about this turn-of-the-century terminal, tours run every Wednesday at 12:30 from the front of Chemical Bank. If you are just passing through, stop at the information booth, which usually is handing out free subway and bus maps—get them while you can. The booth is in the center of the cavernous main hall, with the signs of the zodiac splattered across the ceiling and more terrestrial bodies scurrying across the floor. In the basement is the justly celebrated Oyster Bar. (See *Restaurants* section.)

If the day's too sunny to eat belowstairs, the **Grand Hyatt's** floral atrium next door has a brace of light and airy restaurants which are serenaded by waterfalls and a grand piano at lunchtime.

Across Lexington Avenue from the Hyatt is the beloved **Chrysler Building.** Do take a quick turn about the lobby and peek at the elevators' stunning inlay of art deco work: Each one is different and a gem. The Chrysler's ground floor also houses Con Ed's multimedia energy-saving extravaganza. It's as much fun as a video arcade, and you don't even need quarters to play.

At 220 East 42nd St. is the **New York Daily News Building.** Surrounding the globe in its lobby are a compass and meteorological instruments. The floor is inlaid with distances as well as directions, undoubtedly to remind editors of their stringers scribbling 4,665 miles away in Moscow, 6,463 in Mecca, 9,933 in Sydney.

From hot news, it's a short hop east to a hothouse—the world's largest—in the garden of the **Ford Foundation Building.** The 12-story space is bordered by foundation offices and is kept moist by rainwater from the roof and from steam condensation.

If you prefer greenery of the outdoor variety, walk up the ramp through the atrium to 43rd Street where **Tudor City Park** is nestled to the right.

Beyond the park and down the steps, vigilant on the banks of the East River, are the turquoise tower and the concave chambers of the **United Nations.** Even when there's not an anniversary on, the limos slide effortlessly in and out, unloading their exotic cargo. The hour-long UN tour is quite fascinating and can be caught every 15 minutes, 7 days a week, from 9:15 A.M. to 3:45 P.M. If you plan ahead, try to make a reservation for the delegate's dining room and eat among turbans and fezes. Before you leave, stop at the gift shops, stocked with such from-afar finds as carved flutes from Yugoslavia, batik marionettes from Indonesia, straw shoes from China, and terracotta pottery from the American West. The UN's park is pretty and cool, but the guards will scold you severely if you break out food or Frisbees.

Up 47th Street is the **Japan Society,** which features an array of interesting exhibits, films, and lectures highlighting the arts and letters of Japan and also the achievements of Japanese-American artists and writers. Schedules of upcoming events are available at the information desk just inside the front door. From here wind your way over to Lexington and 45th Street where you'll see Grand Central Post Office (drop off your postcards).

45th Street sneaks between the Pan Am and Helmsley buildings, bypassing the double lanes of Park Avenue traffic. On the ground floor of the former building is the **Trattoria** which extends onto the sidewalk the most spacious (if noisy) outdoor cafe among Midtown restaurants. After 5 you'll find the impoverished but pretty young women from Condé Nast (who bring you *Vogue, Mademoiselle, Self,* etc.) noshing on the Tratt's abundant free happy-hour munchies—fettucini Alfredo, pizzalettes, pasta salad, linguini with mussels—all for the price of a Peroni.

As 45th meets Madison Avenue there is laid a veritable minefield of traps for the junior executive and his/her plastic: **Brooks Brothers** at 346 Madison Ave., replete with correct if uninspired clothing; **Orvis,** at 355 Madison Ave., on 45th Street, evincing outdoorsy tendencies; **Alcott and Andrews,** at 335 Madison Ave., uncomplicated clothes arranged according to color for the woman choosing her toilette on a 10-minute lunch hour; and finally **Paul Stuart,** at 350 Madison Ave.

Paul Stuart is an interesting case: One is almost loath to send a visitor there to be subjected to some of New York's haughtiest salespeople; however, you must brace yourself and put up with it because Paul Stuart does have the most ravishing imported hand-knits, a sumptuous selection of leather belts, bemusing braces, all at prices which will make you certain you've bought the best.

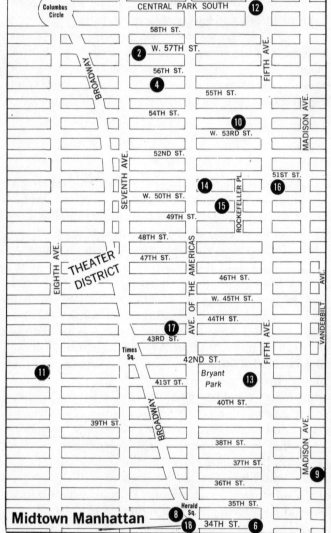

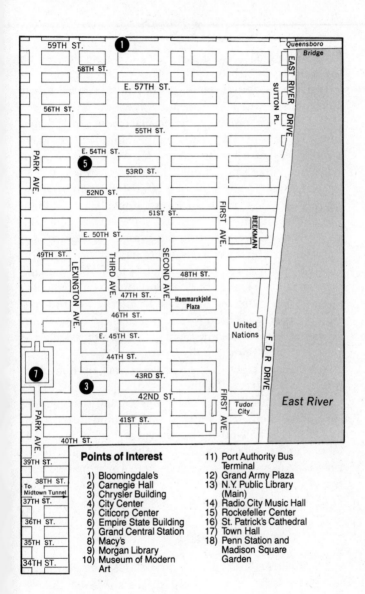

Points of Interest

1) Bloomingdale's
2) Carnegie Hall
3) Chrysler Building
4) City Center
5) Citicorp Center
6) Empire State Building
7) Grand Central Station
8) Macy's
9) Morgan Library
10) Museum of Modern Art
11) Port Authority Bus Terminal
12) Grand Army Plaza
13) N.Y. Public Library (Main)
14) Radio City Music Hall
15) Rockefeller Center
16) St. Patrick's Cathedral
17) Town Hall
18) Penn Station and Madison Square Garden

Nothing like a bout of serious spending to work up an appetite. Which brings us, if we proceed along 45th Street across Fifth Avenue, to the **International Paper Plaza,** and to the all-important subject of lunch.

The green, water-freshened space between 45th and 46th is one of the many more-than-pleasant parks strategically distributed around Midtown to accommodate the people who haven't the means to lunch at "21" or The Four Seasons. The air is far less stuffy in these petite parks. The one at the International Paper Building has lunchtime entertainment, from Broadway to be-bop, more often than not during the summer season. It also has its own gourmet take-away, **Plums,** but the best alfresco comestibles are **Moshe's** felafels from the spanking new cart on the corner of Sixth and 46th. You might also want to check out the Midtown Branch of the **International Center of Photography** just inside the glass windows. Aside from their distinctive exhibits, they sell great postcards and photography books.

After lunch get yourself back on track up Fifth Avenue to 47th Street. To the left is the jewelry center, a block containing several surprising baguettes set among the karats, the first of which is the **Gotham Book Mart,** at 41 West. The Gotham has the largest small-press collection and film book collection in the city. It also is the repository for more of Edward Gorey's marvelously macabre paraphernalia than any bookseller in the world.

47th Street's next little gem is **47th Street Photo.** Up the steep stairs at No. 67 the prices are lower than in Tokyo (no lie) on many items. But the ambience is as much of a draw as the prices. The scene is complete chaos: The salesmen, all Hassidic Jews, shed their black coats, roll up their sleeves, and wrap their curls around their ears, preparing to do heated and high-decibel business. So if you don't need a camera, buy some film, some batteries even—just *go*.

When you return to Fifth Avenue, work your way up to 49th Street to pay your respects to **Saks Fifth Avenue,** then cross the street to the channel gardens sweeping down into the heart of **Rockefeller Center.** In summertime the restaurants spill out into the sunken garden below the Prometheus fountain. In wintertime the garden transforms into an ice rink.

If you're in the mood to stay for a while, you can take the Rock Center walking tour—get a brochure at the info desk at 30 Rockefeller Plaza—or you can take a tour of NBC studios in the middle of the 30 Rock's lobby. Or take in a show at Radio City. Be sure not to miss powdering your nose or straightening your tie in the upstairs deliciously deco lounges.

When you've had your fill of Rockefeller's and Rockettes, ease on up to Fifth and 53rd, a street rife with a diversity of diversions. To the west is the **Museum of Modern Art (MOMA).** The battle still rages, pro and con, over the new facility and its overshadowing condo tower. But whether you're a lover or a loather of the building, its contents are a must-see. Everyone's favorites are here, from Pissarro to Picasso. One of the city's most juicy juxtapositionings is the view from the **Phillip Johnson Gallery** upstairs. The architect has donated a formidable collection of works, installed in a gallery through the windows of which his granite Chippendale AT&T Building blushes pink against the sky.

On the corner of Fifth Ave. and 53rd is **St. Thomas Church.** Often overlooked in favor of its more famous brother, **St. Patrick's,** down the avenue, St. Thomas's interior is highlighted by a magnificent ceiling-high altar screen, and its boys choir—the finest this side of Vienna

—frequently gives concerts, in addition to singing on Sundays.

Across the avenue at 1 East 53rd is the collection of another modern art: **The Museum of Broadcasting.** Three dollars gets you in to see the latest exhibits and entitles you to enjoy up to an hour's worth of any of the 20,000 radio and TV programs they have on file. You'd like to relive the Beatles on Ed Sullivan? The Who on the Smothers Brothers? Olivier in *King Lear?* Lucy in hot water? They're all here, but the consoles are reserved fast, so come as close to the noon opening time as possible.

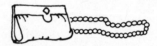

At the corner of Fifth and 56th is the store for **Steuben** glass. Not only will they sell you crystal tortoises, bowls, apples, and candelabra, they also have a gallery of exquisite sculpted and carved glass at the back of the store.

Across 56th Street is the **Trump Tower:** Donald's trumped-up version of your mall at home, in which instead of building out, he built up. The Trump Tower's most outstanding feature is its six-story atrium with a waterfall cascading down rose-colored marble. Much more pleasant (and certainly less draining on pocket and patience) is the **IBM** atrium, through **Bonwit Teller** on Madison Avenue. IBM has planted graceful bamboo through which light shimmers softly. The Juilliard School presents concerts several times weekly at 12:30 or 5 P.M.; check the bulletin board for upcoming events.

Beyond the glass doors to the left is the IBM museum. Admission is free to their various exhibits of art and science. In the lobby be sure to have a go at the New York Culture Guide, a computerized reference. The consoles offer a do-it-yourself video tour of what to see and do in the five boroughs, crossreferenced according to location, title, interest, etc.

As you leave the IBM Building, turn left on 57th Street, where you are confronted with a British invasion (with a soupçon of French thrown in) across the street. **Laura Ashley** is two floors of ruffled shirts, jumpers, and petticoats. **Jaeger** has somewhat more understated threads, for the Anglophilic sophisticate. **Hermès** sells its signature silk equestrian scarves, 36 × 36, for $140; men's silk ties for $65. If you are seriously of the horsey set, you can dress your mount in a Hermès saddle for $2,000—stirrups will set you back an extra $295. **Burberry's** sells their raincoats lined with beige, red, white, and black plaid to ladies for $490, to gents for $460. The walls are decorated with deer racks and hunting prints to give you that tally-ho feeling.

What self-respecting modern romantic could say no to an engagement ring in a demure blue box from **Tiffany and Co.**? The grande dame of diamonds is ensconced at 57th and Fifth, but don't even think about going there at lunchtime, especially during the prenuptial rush around May. You'll wait what seems like hours for a salesperson who will enact for you Tiffany's incomprehensible and irritating stock procurement procedure: an arcane system for delivering your package, involving endless phone calls and form filling-out. Best to pick up your wedding gifts some morning in February.

By this time you're probably ready to sit one out, and one of the most relaxing and comfortable seats in the city is to be found in a **horse-drawn carriage,** waiting at Grand Army Plaza to trot you through Central Park. The trip might at first seem the height of tacky tourism, but it really is a lot of fun and less expensive than you might think—$17 for the first half hour, $5 for each additional 15 minutes.

A somewhat more warming respite can be had in the form of afternoon tea. Who else but the queen herself, Leona Helmsley, would reinstate the tradition at her **Palace Hotel,** at Madison and 50th? Several others have followed Leona's lead and, come 5 o'clock, are brimful and Oolong and Earl Grey, scones and finger sandwiches: the **St. Regis,** Fifth at 55th; **The Plaza,** Fifth and 59th; The **Waldorf-Astoria,** Park and 50th. If you prefer something more spirited, the atrium of the **Parker Meridien,** 118 West 59th St., serves up cocktails and piano music, and the **Drake Hotel**, Park and 56th, has one of the world's only champagne bars where you can choose from among 10 brands of bubbly.

Evening in Midtown is the stuff dreams are made (and fortunes unmade) on: the latest of Broadway theater at 8, followed by a sumptuous dinner at **Lutèce** or **La Grenouille.** If you're still game for more, the only way to top drama and dining is to be literally on top of the town. Midtown is full of high-in-the-sky options for a stellar end to your evening.

Nirvana at One Times Square overlooks the hustle and bustle in an Indian atmosphere (great spot for happy-hour sunsets, too); **The Rainbow Room** at Rockefeller Center features dancing till dawn, to Panama Francis and the Savoy Sultans. And finally, a little off the beaten track but therefore less trafficked by out-of-towners, is the **Beekman Tower,** First and 49th, situated well to the east, so you can sit outside in summer and look back on the lights of Midtown igniting the heavens for miles around.

UPPER EAST SIDE

The Upper East Side has long been the province of the "haves" in Manhattan. In the early 20th century, the Carnegies, Vanderbilts, Astors, and others of their well-heeled ilk parked their fortunes along Fifth Avenue. Some of their stately pleasure homes have been commissioned as museums, in which you can wander about and sense the high life enjoyed by former owners. Although apartment houses have superseded most of the mansions on the avenues, the cross streets in the 70s and 80s are bordered by some simply fabulous, still privately owned houses.

The Upper East Side has become one of the last reserves of that vanishing breed: the Lady of Leisure. On weekdays you can spot these rare birds perambulating down Madison Avenue, off to lunch at Le Cirque or to be revived at **Elizabeth Arden,** or to hunt down a new hat at a favorite milliner.

This is not to say there's no new blood in the neighborhood. Second and Third Avenues are jammed with bars and restaurants catering to the grande dames' progeny, just escaped from Brown or Stanford, cutting loose in the first rush of postgraduate freedom.

Even these youngbloods' taste has patrician tendencies, and the Upper East Side provides a plentitude of goods and services to coax the Park Avenue crowd into blowing the cobwebs off their Old Money. The galleries representing the most sought-after artists (both present and past) have largely decamped from 57th Street and reinstated themselves uptown. The designers of Europe fly in their fashions fresh from London, Paris, Milan, to the boutiques along Madison Avenue. From 71st to 104th streets, museums, with a quality and variety of collections unequaled elsewhere on the planet, cater to the cultural interests of the masses by day, host fund-raisers for high-society by night.

It is impossible to design a day-long tour of the Upper East Side because you could easily spend a day—or week or month—exploring a single one of its dozen museums. The following constitutional will take you to most of the interesting spots; how you choose to apportion your time there is up to you.

Beginning with what's new at 75th and Madison is the **Whitney Museum of American Art,** famous for exploring the works of popular modern artists—Edward Hopper, Nam June Paik, Walt Disney—and bringing to light many new luminaries. There is a pleasant cafe (outdoors in summer) in the basement.

If it's sweets of the palate you crave, you might take a quick nip up to Madison and 78th, where you'll find **G & M Pastries** for melt-in-your mouth goodies, or **St. Ambroeus** for the city's best gelati—of an even more ephemeral nature. You deserve a little indulgence to balance out all this culture.

70th Street houses a brace of fine galleries: **Knoedler** at No. 19 and **Hirschl and Adler** at No. 21. Knoedler specializes in American painting from the 18th century on. Hirschl and Adler specializes in European old masters and 20th century art.

If you need a little encouragement to start a gallery *chez vous,* proceed to the **Frick Collection** on the corner of Fifth Avenue. Here is a private art collection—steel magnate Henry Clay Frick's—mind-boggling in scope and style. Because it was built as a residence as well as a gallery, the Frick has a somewhat less reserved atmosphere than its relatives up Fifth Avenue. Surrounding an indoor garden fountain are rooms containing masterpieces.

Returning to Madison Avenue, you may want to make another detour, this time to the east to Park Ave. and 70th St. where stands the **Asia Society.** This striking structure of Oklahoma red granite houses some of the Rockefellers' vast collection of Asian art, in addition to visiting exhibits. They have an extensive lecture and film schedule for the make-mine-Ming set.

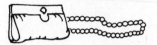

Back on Madison, the exotic Orient gives way to exotic Europe. The bouquet of boutiques sweeping through the 70s speaks with many tongues to many tastes. If Italian pleases you, you can revel in romanza at the stores for **Missoni** (No. 836), **Giorgio Armani** (No. 813), **Gianni Versace** (No. 808), and **Emanuel Ungaro** (No. 803). If you like the French styles, **Kenzo** is at No. 824, **Sonia Rykiel** is at No. 792, **Lanvin** is at No. 701. If you fancy a bit of Brit, you can be shod by **Joan and David** or sweatered by **Joseph Tricot.**

Just off the avenue at 19 East 65th St. is **Rita Ford Music Boxes.** Perhaps you'll run into Johnny Cash picking up a custom-made box of one of his standards for June Carter. Or maybe Jim Henson will be buying a tinkling rendition of "Rubber Ducky" for Miss Piggy. Music makers and lovers come here to choose a gift from the $18,000 1890s Leipzig Polyphon or the dancing demoiselles, or the chirping birds in their gilded cage.

The gilded age awaits you at the Manhattan version of **Maxims,** transplanted from the Rue Royale in the entirety of its exquisite excess. (See *Restaurants* chapter.)

If your purse allows you only to drink a Rothschild rather than to live like one, you can pick up a Mouton Cadet decorated by Andy Warhol or John Huston at **Sherry-Lehman,** 679 Madison. The ambience is reminiscent of one of the baron's own wine caves. The same firm has been selling spirits since Prohibition and does a brisk 100,000-case business annually. Customers have run the gamut from Harry Truman to Craig Claiborne to Mick Jagger. They publish a monthly chat sheet and catalogue, and will deliver free anywhere in New York State.

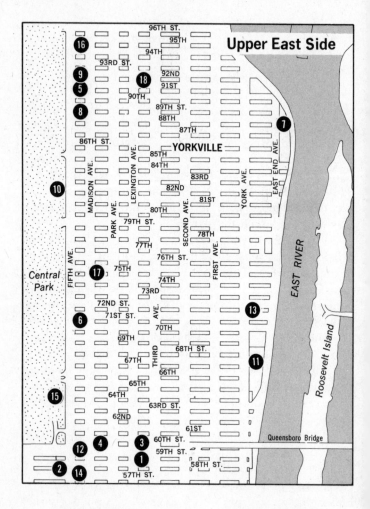

Points of Interest

1) Alexander's
2) Bergdorf Goodman
3) Bloomingdale's
4) Christie's
5) Cooper-Hewitt Museum
6) Frick Collection
7) Gracie Mansion
   (Mayor's residence)
8) Guggenheim Museum

9) Jewish Museum
10) Metropolitan Museum of Art
11) Rockefeller University
12) F.A.O. Schwarz
13) Sotheby Parke Bernet
14) Tiffany
15) Central Park Zoo
16) International Center
    of Photography
17) Whitney Museum
18) YM-YWHA

Now, of course, you'll need something to sop up all that bubbly, so proceed to 29 East 60th to the **Caviarteria.** Louis Sobel has been selling sturgeon progeny-to-be for over 30 years and his prices and quality will have you buying up beluga like there's no tomorrow. They will also supply you with crackers (although they recommend your own light toast), smoked Scotch salmon, and pâté.

Make a quick right then left to 59th Street (between Park and Lexington avenues), on the north side of which is **Fiorucci's,** Italy's own answer to kitsch. Upstairs is a new wig department; downstairs check out the sale stuff and the postcards.

The American version of this philosophy waits to bowl you over down the street. Proceed at your own risk. You might have thought the zoo was several blocks to the east in Central Park, but set one paw in **Bloomingdale's** and you'll be subsumed in the mercantile jungle. (See *Shopping* section.)

Make your escape out the back door to a semblance of sanity down 60th Street. At No. 225 is **Serendipity,** which scoops up the mincingest waiters and most mountainous fudge sundaes in Manhattan. Also luscious are frozen moccachino in the summer or frothy mocco-cocoa in the winter.

At No. 229 is the shop for **Liberty of London,** stacked with bolts of its famous soft sheen cotton prints at $15 per yard. You can buy their romantic posies or rich paisleys wrapped around date books, address books, or made into pizzazzy neckties and feminine dresses. The perfect gift is and always has been a Liberty silk square, $40.

One block north and two blocks east at 421 East 61st St. is the **Abigail Adams Smith House.** Gone through several metamorphoses, as a stable, then a tavern and Salvation Army soup kitchen, the 1799 house of John Adams's daughter is a cache of early American antiques and has a bright swatch of garden during the green months. Open Mondays–Fridays; closed in August.

Retrace your steps to Second Avenue and head north, passing through Yorkville, where eastern Europeans (Germans, Czechoslovakians, Hungarians) set up shop when they arrived in several waves, beginning in the mid–19th century.

One of the shops still redolent with the scent of the old country is **Paprika Weiss,** at 1546 Second Ave., between 80th and 81st streets. The Weisses have been supplying the neighborhood with spaetzle, tarhanya, orzo nokedli for four generations. Their specialty is spices, spices, and spices. Ed Weiss travels the globe sending home sackfuls of Indonesian pepper, cinnamon from mainland China, maracaibo from Venezuela, and, of course, paprika from Hungary.

Up Second Avenue at the corner of 84th is a new edition of old-country flavor, only this time the gusto is Italian. **Caffé Biffi** is pretty pink marble and brass, with curvilinear windows allowing you to sip your cappuccino or one of their wide selection of aperitifs while watching the world go by.

East down 84th Street is a more home-grown type joint. Drop in **Elsie Renne Oke Doke Bar** at No. 307, a quirky and cozy pub with a welcome downtown feel squeezed in here in the northern part of the island. Continue your 84th Street dalliance across the way at **Action Comics,** at No. 318, floor-to-ceiling with Captain Marvel and Wonder Woman and Spiderman.

Enjoy the fine rowhouses gracing the sidewalks of 84th as you wend your way eastward to the river and Carl Schurz Park, one of the prettiest, least pedestrian-packed green places you'll find. Here is **Gracie Mansion,** home of Mayor Ed Koch. Hizzoner's no fool: the pretty 1799 canary yellow Federal mansion was built on a former fort site by a Scottish merchant. Tours of the interior run sporadically from March to November. Call for information, 570–4751.

As you begin your hike back toward Central Park, pause to admire Henderson Place, 86th to 87th streets on East End Avenue. These are 24 of 32 homes remaining, originally built on John Jacob Astor land, preserved to give you a sense of how the neighborhood looked brand new in 1882.

Working your way west across 86th Street you might want to drop in one of the German specialty shops and restaurants that sell or serve records, handicrafts, kaffee, and küchen from the homeland. When you at last reach Fifth Avenue, you'll see the imposing facade of the **Metropolitan Museum of Art,** two blocks south.

After your trek, take five on Fifth: There's no better place to see New York—nay, the world—go by than from the Met's steps. The warm weather brings mimes, magicians, and comics to entertain the assembled art lovers. People laze, sun, chatter; toddlers and matrons make their way gingerly up the stairs. When you get to the top, you know you've arrived.

Where to begin to suggest what to see in this mammoth collection? The Impressionists are upstairs to the right; arms and armor are down the main floor passage to the right; the costume exhibit is through the Egyptian Wing and downstairs. If you are as bewildered as you should be by the embarrassment of choices, ask the people at the info desk in the center of the main hall to suggest something to your taste. The popularity of major exhibits often requires advance-purchase tickets at an additional fee. If you have the good fortune to be here at Christmastime, ensconced in the medieval hall is the museum's Christmas tree and crèche, a baroque beauty whose figures were fashioned by 18th century Neapolitan artisans. All year round the museum sponsors lectures, films, musical programs; get a schedule while you're at the info desk.

The Metropolitan is the southern parenthesis of Museum Mile: twenty-odd blocks of densely packed culture along Fifth Avenue. As mentioned, you could easily spend your entire visit to New York sampling the spectrum of art, architecture, history, and design splashed up the avenue. Highlights to hit along the way are the **Guggenheim,** at 80th Street, Frank Lloyd Wright's bequest to the city, hosting shows of contemporary works and housing its own impressive permanent collection. It's tough to be a work of art in this building—the spiral gallery's downhill execution constantly upstages the paintings trying to hold their own as they hang on its walls.

The **Cooper-Hewitt,** at 90th Street, is the Smithsonian Institution's National Museum of Design made at home in Andrew Carnegie's former digs. The museum has its own collection of design feats, but most especially is a favorite for its continuously clever, unorthodox rotating exhibits, an impressive 15 a year, which keep the curators scurrying. Every time you come, it's completely different. In summertime there are concerts in Carnegie's pretty, peaceful backyard.

The entrance to the **International Center of Photography** is just in off Fifth on 94th Street. Housed in another mansion, the ICOP's walls support this century's leading exponents of portrait, documentary, landscape, experimental photography. They have a video screening room and offer a provocative list of lectures and classes on still and motion pictures.

The **Museum of the City of New York,** at 103rd Street, traces the history of the city from the time when the white men supposedly bought the Isle of the Manhattoes for $24 worth of trinkets; back in the days when Peter Stuyvesant declared a resolution to all contractors "to complete the palisades around the port of Nieuw Amsterdam in order to protect it against the hogs."

If the daylight hours are not numerous enough for you to explore the Mile as exhaustively as you'd like, the Metropolitan, Guggenheim, Cooper-Hewitt, ICOP, and Whitney museums are open till 8 P.M. on Tuesdays (several waive their admission fee at this time), so you can stretch your art appreciation into the evening.

UPPER WEST SIDE

When *New York* magazine did its cover story on this neighborhood, they called it "The Yupper West Side." Half the residents giggled in delight, reading tales of their exploits along Columbus Avenue. Half the residents cringed at being reminded of the chi-chi creeping ever farther up Broadway.

The neighborhood is a playground for financially solvent, college-educated young adults. Acting as buffer zones on either side are Central Park to the east and Riverside Park to the west. The two parks provide a spacious, outdoor, surprisingly exclusive health club: Upper West Siders are generally fit and thirsty. They work hard, they run hard, they drink hard. So what's not to like?

There is also a certain amount of satisfaction to be derived from having **Lincoln Center** at one's doorstep (between 62nd and 66th streets west of Broadway, to be exact). Lincoln Center is a festive place just about any time of year. Its trinity of soaring '60s arcades have held up surprisingly well as a continuously pleasant public space.

During the day tourists snap shots by the fountain; it's the urban answer to Old Faithful. In the evening the plaza is aglitter with exquisitely dressed, shod, perfumed New Yorkers rushing to catch curtains.

In summertime things are especially lively here, with Lincoln Center Out-of-Doors importing free programs of dance, music, and drama at lunchtime, after work around 5:30, and in the evening. Cafés roost outside Avery Fisher Hall, providing alfresco libation. The New York Film Festival runs in September at Alice Tully Hall; tickets are tough, but possible, to come by. The Big Apple Circus, much more fun than a barrel of monkeys, sets up tent in Damrosch Park (to the left of the opera house) in the spring and the Christmas season. City Ballet's *Nutcracker* and Masterwork Chorus's *Messiah* at Christmas, and the Met's *Parsival* at Easter are perennial favorites.

Permanently available and entertaining is the **Library of the Performing Arts,** where you can listen to a massive collection of classical, jazz, folk, and Broadway recordings or watch tapes of PBS's *Live From Lincoln Center* programs on the video. If you don't have tickets, standing room at the Met is $5 and $8—you can usually grab a $40 orchestra seat by Act II. Finally, there is the Lincoln Center Tour which takes you onstage and into the bowels of the complex, to costume, property, and scenery shops. Call for schedules, 877–1800.

An alternate world of entertainment is found at **Star Magic** at 73rd and Amsterdam. The store is a minimart for the occult, science fiction, and science fact. You can float through waves of mesmerizing music, be lulled into snapping up Einstein postcards, tarot cards, hologram jewelry, telescopes, which will be explained to you by equally spacey salespeople with mandalas and orange hair.

Turn down 73rd Street and float across to Columbus Avenue at the corner of which is **Fizzazz,** No. 280. Fizzazz bubbles over with Coca-Cola fashions which you can preview on their do-it-yourself fashion show monitors and big screens. You touch the screen to find out prices, fabric content, colors, and sizes of the carbonate-inspired clothes.

This is an appropriate introduction to the Columbus Avenue experience—a strip of self-conscious funkiness. The best time to see the sights is on the weekend, when the residents are home from Madison Avenue and Wall Street. You'll remark on the number of adult amusements here along the route to help them relax.

There are the **Last Wound-up** (No. 290), or **Mythology** (No. 312), both grown-up toy stores. Unwind at the former, which sells sneakers that walk by themselves, a detailed ambulatory brontosaurus, an Empire State-scaling King Kong. Mythology catches the spillover from the Museum of Natural History in its web of modern

design books, antique toys and games, and a full comple-
ment of transformers.

One block east, on Central Park West between 76th
and 77th, is the **New York Historical Society,** which
examines American artists and artisans, generally, and
the city's and region's pasts, particularly.

The **Museum of Natural History,** Central Park
West and 79th, is the place to get kids (or the kid in you)
excited about museums (anew). Many of the displays are
taxidermy gone wild—tableaux of elephants and hum-
mingbirds, blue whales, and earthworms. The dinosaur
rooms are still the most jaw-dropping sights around—if
you don't count the Hayden Planetarium. Plan to spend
a long visit at the Natural History; it's open till 9 P.M. on
Wednesdays, Saturdays, and Sundays.

Head back to Columbus Avenue for some animal
behavior studies of your own. The row of shops behind
the museum is a good place to see just what these Yup-
pers are up to. On the corner of 81st is **Charivari Workshop,** where are sold fashions even more bizarre than in
their regular store over on Amsterdam and 79th. Gary
the manager says, "This is a testing ground for newer
designers and ideas; that's why we called it 'Workshop.'"
Here you'll find a crushed velvet smoking jacket, a crimson velour fez, plastic silver oxfords.

At 487 Columbus things are a tad more down-to-
earth at **Handblock,** which is afroth with cotton-print
quilts, tablecloths, covers for design-your-own pillows,
and a line of clothing. The store demonstrates the finer
things that can be done with India's textiles.

On the next block is **Lucy's,** the Cal-Mex vortex of
the neighborhood. Margarita aficionados are fairly wall-
to-wall after 9:30 P.M., should you care to have a chat with
the locals, and the T-shirts are pretty cute.

Turn down 85th and walk to Amsterdam, where a
block north at No. 531 you'll find **A Show of Hands.**
Open 7 days a week, the store is a crafts cooperative, but

don't picture pot holders and papier-mâché. Artisans from the city donate their time and treasures to the store: unusual, idiosyncratic jewelry, pottery, blown glass, weaving, silk batik scarves.

Across 86th Street at 541 and 551 Amsterdam are **Barney Greengrass** and the **Popover Café,** respectively. A brace of restaurants to warm the cockles of any serious bruncher's heart. Barney Greengrass is an ethnic delight featuring eggs with lox and cream cheese, bagels and the like. The Popover Café is a veritable nest of WASPishness. Both places are very popular and are known to sport as much as an hour wait during busy brunchtimes. Both are inexpensive.

Back on Broadway, at 80th, is **Zabars,** nerve center of the neighborhood. Everybody who is anybody is here stocking up for partying or cruising for a date if they're partyless. You can join the fray if so inclined or get some picnic fixings and scramble back out the door.

After you've stopped and shopped and supped, continue your quest for the waterside by heading westward down 86th Street toward the Hudson and the continent of North America directly across (New Yorkers are often wont to make the distinction between themselves and others living on the land mass). You'll eventually come upon **Riverside Park.** To the south is the **79th Street Boat Basin:** People actually tie up in the Hudson, and some even beat Upper West Side skyrocketing rents by living on their boats. Riverside Park is a stretch of green between the water and Riverside Drive, sometimes bisected by the Henry Hudson Parkway, stretching north beyond the George Washington Bridge. It is the most spectacular park in the city in the spring, strewn with pink and white apple and cherry blossoms.

Stroll up toward the bridge, crossing under the highway and up a steep incline to the promenade at the north end of which is the People's Garden. During the growing season, there's usually one of the neighborhood volun-

teer gardeners, weeding, fertilizing, pruning the one cir-
cular and two oblong beds of flowers that fairly hum with
color and bumblebees from early spring to late autumn.
Feel free to feast on your Zabar's grub on one of the
benches or the cushiony lawn behind. Walk north along
the path, which is interrupted by the roadway at 95th
Street. Turn right up 95th past Riverside Drive and West
End Avenue.

On the south side of 95th is an archway bracketed by
two streetlamps. If you crane your neck upward, you can
glimpse the tops of the houses of **Pomander Walk.** Unfortunately they locked the gate recently, but you can still
get a sense of the quaint row of houses which look a bit
like Amsterdam.

On the corner of 95th and Broadway is **Symphony
Space,** which welcomes performances, from opera to
avant-garde. One of their best events is the annual free
marathon reading of James Joyce's *Ulysses* on Bloomsday.
Each June 16 some great names (and voices) from theater
and films narrate Leopold Bloom's odyssey through
Dublin on this date in 1904.

Up Broadway through the 90s and into the 100s is
the beginning of Columbia University's sphere of influence. You'll notice it as the area gives way to boutiques
and bars vying for space with the bodegas.

As you turn the corner to the right on 112th Street,
you will be arrested by the awe-inspiring sight of the
Cathedral of St. John the Divine at the far end of the
street. This is the largest cathedral outside of St. Peter's
in Rome; however, it envelops a broad constituency of
philosophies. Whether you are Episcopalian (like the
congregation) or Buddhist or atheist, you might like to
drop by on a Sunday morning. The choir is first-rate, the
lights are all turned on, the air is perfumed by incense,
and the sermon is given by guest speakers whose numbers include the Reverend Jesse Jackson, architect Philip
Johnson, Bishop Desmond Tutu, Governor Mario
Cuomo. One of the best Sundays to come is the first one
in October for the celebration of the Feast of St. Francis,
when people bring their dogs and parrots, the police
escort their mounts, circuses and zoos send their llamas
and elephants down the center aisle to be blessed.

After visiting the cathedral, stop in at the **Hungarian Pastry Shop,** across Amsterdam at 111th Street, for European coffees and melt-in-your-mouth pastries (angel wings are the best).

The **Columbia University** campus stretches from Broadway to Amsterdam, beginning at 114th Street and dwindling down about eight blocks north. There is always music, theater, film, and lectures to the public each week. In December New Yorkers hunting for unusual gifts find just the thing at the WBAI Crafts Fair (655–4465) held at the student center, Ferris Booth Hall, at the southwest corner of the campus.

Evenings on the Upper West Side are, of course, made magic by a concert of the Philharmonic, an opera at the Met, a ballet danced on the stage of the New York State Theater. But culture abounds up here in the northlands. **Riverside Church,** at 120th Street, sponsors a dance festival from spring through summer; bound-for-Broadway hits have their tryouts at the **Promenade Theatre** on 76th Street.

Although many Upper West Siders take it for granted, a large number of movies from classic to commercial are screened in Upper West Side movie houses. Around Lincoln Center there are usually a dozen of the latest European, South American, and Asian export pieces at the **Lincoln Plaza Cinemas, Cinema Studio,** and the **Embassy.** Hollywood blockbusters debut at the **84th Street Six** and the **Metro.** One word of advice: People in Manhattan still go out to the movies, so don't be disappointed in your film-going by arriving 10 minutes before showtime to find a long line or sold-out seating.

Lower midtown

Lower Midtown is a convenient term, a catchall in which to toss the various neighborhoods between the Hudson and the East rivers, from 42nd Street to 14th Street. Heading south from 42nd, you find to the west the garment district, central control for what's affectionately known locally as the Rag Trade—surprisingly enough, NYC's largest industry by far. On the east side is Murray Hill descending to 34th Street—largely residential. South of the garment district, Chelsea begins roughly at 23rd Street: an up-and-coming neighborhood, with restaurants lining the avenues and brownstones lining the streets. East of Chelsea in the middle of the island is the photo district where the world's most celebrated shutterbugs set up their studios. East of there, on the far side of Manhattan, is Gramercy Park, also largely residential with the exception of the medical centers which front the East River.

Begin at the **Morgan** (John Pierpont, that is) **Library** at Madison Ave. and 36th St. J.P. would settle for nothing less than the best in the world at the bank or at home, so he charged McKim, Mead and White to build a bungalow for his books and himself in 1906.

The collection includes *First Folios* of Shakespeare, handwritten manuscripts of Dickens, which are on display at various times, along with exhibitions of illuminated manuscripts, children's books, and the literary like. The rooms are richly appointed, with antiques, Renaissance paintings, and thousands of leather-bound, gold-tooled volumes. (Closed Mondays and all of August.)

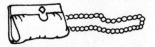

If you'd like to purchase some classic finery for yourself, downhill at Madison, between 34th and 35th, is **B. Altman & Co.,** one of New York's venerable Fifth Avenue furnishers. Sneaking through the back door on

Madison enables you to escape the crowds at the Fifth Avenue entrance and enjoy the store's plush red carpet rolled out for you, illuminated by massive crystal chandeliers. Ladies Who Lunch still do so upstairs at the Charleston Gardens; its ante-bellum mural and gloved-and-hatted customers remind you of a time when life was a little more gracious.

Diagonally across from Altman's front doors is the **Empire State Building.** One backward tilt of the head will acquaint you with the altitude which made Fay Wray so apprehensive as she ascended, clasped in Kong's furry fist. We suggest going to the top by elevator rather than by ape, a feat easily accomplished for a mere $3.25 any time from 9:30 A.M. to 11:20 P.M.

No less spectacular than the 80-mile view from above is the view in the lobby, with its perfectly matched marble and deco appointments. You might also want to stop in the **Guinness World Records Exhibit Hall** ($3), where you can compare the height of Mt. Everest to the Empire State Building or the world's largest locust swarm to Manhattan Island.

Out the north entrance and across the street, at 27 West 34th, is a little-known secret: the restaurant of the **New York Restaurant School.** The culmination of the school's grueling 20-week program is working in their fine, sensibly priced dining room on the fourth floor. Lunch and dinner are served Monday through Friday by a staff of soon-to-be graduates who rotate stations, from busboy to maître d' to pastry chef. Reservations are necessary (947–7105).

At the juncture of 34th Street, Sixth Avenue, and Broadway is Herald Square (more like two triangles, actually); on the west side at 34th Street are the **Herald Center** and **Macy's.** The former is new (reputedly owned by Imelda Marcos), and not nearly as nice as the latter.

These days most people love Macy's for The Cellar, its basementful of edibles, appliances, and shops for children and teenagers. Take the wooden escalators two-thirds of the way back in the store downstairs to sample the savories that the world's largest department store has in store. Macy's goes on the must-visit list come spring-time, when the entire main floor is ablaze with a spec-

tacular flower show, and of course the famous parade
drops Santa off at the door every Thanksgiving.

Turn left off 34th Street on Seventh Avenue, past
Madison Square Garden (pick up some Rangers or
Knicks tix, if you like). Continue west on 33rd Street
where at No. 450 you'll find the **Sky Rink.** No kidding,
you can lace up some skates and do figure-eights on the
ice 16 stories above the street.

Cross Eighth Avenue and continue westward along
26th Street past the warehouses to Eleventh Avenue
where Matthew Reich, from the Bronx, has just started
doing something nobody's been doing much in Manhattan for years. Reich has moved his operation south from
Utica, so now **New Amsterdam Beer and Ale** are being
brewed right in the city for which they were named. In
the tradition of the great European breweries, the operation includes a lot of pride and devotion to detail and
luckily also includes, like its continental counterparts,
free ten-minute tours at 3 and 5 P.M., culminating in a
tasting at the Tap Room restaurant out front.

Get yourself to 270 West 11th St. where Joe Bach
has parked the **American Classic Garage,** a combination
club, showroom, ice-cream parlor, and movie theater (a
drive-in indoors). You'll recognize the building by the
bas-relief Chevrolets in huge effigy decorating the exteri-
or. You'll now want to take to the water, so roll on down
to Pier 62 at 23rd Street on the Hudson where you can
catch a cruise to have you rolling on the river. The *Em-
press of New York* and the *Riveranda* leave at noon for a
two-hour luncheon ($22) or at 7 for a 3-hour dinner
($45) voyage. (Two Sunday brunch tours depart at 12:-
30.) The trips are extremely popular, so you'd best book
well in advance (929–7090), although if you're feeling
lucky, you may be able to wrangle a same-day stowaway
booking. All cruises have live music (and dancing at dinner) as the boats motor down the Hudson, around the tip

of Manhattan past the Statue of Liberty, up the East River, then turn around to return to Pier 62.

You might want to take a break to get back your land legs at the **Empire Diner** on the corner of 22nd St. and Eleventh Ave. Open 24 hours, the Empire is a souped-up, cosmo version of your local hash house, except they sell booze, have live piano music, and cater to celebrities of varying degrees and dispositions at around 4:30 A.M.

Cross 22nd, turn right down Tenth Avenue to 20th Street, and continue eastward through these peaceful streets, the prettiest in Chelsea. When you reach Eighth Avenue, walk south to 17th Street, pausing by whatever windows strike your fancy. If you tarry at **Rick's Lounge,** get a frozen margarita, complete with parasol and plastic mermaids swimming in the pink froth.

At 17th Street walk to **Barney's** at Seventh Avenue. This is the only serious department store downtown and the only department store more seriously devoted to men than women.

As 16th Street crosses Fifth Avenue, **Folklorica** is to your left at 89 Fifth. The store's caravans comb the exotic climes of the world and pack back to New York textiles, jewelry, woodcarving and basketry of rare design and quality. To your right on Fifth is **Royal Silk,** behind the diagonal glass at No. 79. The store is stocked with a spectrum of colors and styles in silk at polyester prices.

Beyond Fifth Avenue, 16th Street runs into Union Square. Formerly the only herb you could buy here was the smokable variety, but now on Wednesdays, Fridays, and Saturdays, the park presents edible herbs, courtesy of Manhattan's largest green market. Farmers bring veggies, cider, fruit pies from New Jersey, fresh fish from Long Island, flowers from upstate—it's a taste of the country in the city. If all this puts you in an outdoorsy frame of mind, you can mosey up Broadway to **Paragon** sports outfitters and get yourself geared up for whatever adventures you have in mind. They have a wide wilderness stock, especially sleeping bags and tents on the second floor.

If you prefer indoor adventuring, two of the pleasantest pubs you could ask for sit on 18th Street—tin-ceilinged, tile-floored, convivial-atmosphered. The **Old Town** is the lesser-known of the two, and prefers to remain that way. They've already turned down one offer to film there. **Pete's Tavern,** at the corner of Irving Place, is especially nice when decorated for Christmas or, when the weather permits, for sidewalk café-ing.

Irving Place is so named for Washington Irving, who chronicled the jejune metropolis hilariously in *Knicker-bocker's New York,* and lived in the brick building with the wrought iron balconies at No. 40.

Up to the north is Gramercy Park, an enclave of civility and refinement. The green square behind the fence can only be used by those fortunate residents who possess a key to the gate. On the south side at No. 15 is the Tilden House, which is the headquarters of the **National Arts Club** and the **Poetry Society.** There is a gallery upstairs open to the public, and they sponsor occasional poetry readings. Now the place is mostly a private club for businessmen who want a bar with culture and quiet.

Walk west from Gramercy Park to Third Avenue then up to 23rd Street. Turn right and you'll see the **School of Visual Arts** at 209 23rd St. Their gallery features the work of students and alumni. Monday–Friday from 9 to 5; Friday and Saturday 10–4.

At 34th on the East River are two heliports, the farther south of which is *Island Helicopters,* which operates sightseeing trips around the island. $25 will get you a 5–7-minute hop down the East River and back; $75, a 20–22-minute circuit of the city. They are open 9 A.M.–5 P.M. and 7–9 P.M., seven days a week, depending on the weather. No reservations are necessary: just show up, cash (or credit card) in hand, and they'll whisk you aloft.

As you no doubt have gathered from the foregoing, the space between 42nd and 14th streets covers a lot of ground and contains a lot of atmospheres. The choice of nightlife presents an equally provocative eclecticism. (See *Nightlife* chapter.)

GREENWICH VILLAGE

To a visitor it may seem a bit preposterous for this city, with its reputation for sinful sophistication, to call a portion of itself something as quaint as "Greenwich Village." But to a New Yorker this swatch of space, officially demarking the geographical and psychological beginnings of Downtown, is the city at its most charming. The tree-lined sidestreets bordered by brownstones, with their sweeping stairs and neat gardens, bring the metropolis down to size. Undoubtedly the Village will make a believer out of you too. Once you've enjoyed the nonchalant chic of its cafes, you'll think twice before paying Uptown prices for surly waiters again. Once you've strolled its streets discovering one-of-a-kind shops, the indoor mall will never be the same.

If you're stalking the wild Bohemian suffering for his art in a cold-water garret, his current address is the East Village or Hoboken: The writers and artists who now live in the old West Village frequent the *New York Times'* best-seller list or grace the walls of the Whitney Museum. As one of the Village's last vagrant poets, Bob Dylan, observed, "The Times They Are A-Changing."

But while they're forced to squat elsewhere, intellectuals—both established and aspiring—still flock to the West Village as their traditional mecca. The minute the weather warms up, the cafes tumble out onto the sidewalk, sparkling with conversations running the gamut from the far left to the extreme right. Thinkers of all persuasions have been tamed to tolerant coexistence here: *Forbes Magazine,* that conservative bastion which proudly proclaims itself "Capitalist Tool," at 60 Fifth Ave., is six doors away from the *Nation,* that liberal publication which refers to "capitalist tools" only in the pejorative sense.

But don't worry, you needn't concern yourself with the cosmos to appreciate the Village's various delights. So prepare yourself to be bewitched by sleepy lanes and sizzling clubs, old-world charm and big-city vitality.

The Village's dizzying extremes are counterbalanced by the more human scale here: the buildings, not presuming to scrape the sky, are content just to sit under it. And you'll want to do likewise if you find yourself in **Washington Square Park** on a sunny afternoon. Wrapped around by New York University, the park features free entertainment. Pushers and punks mingle with poodles and Ph.D. candidates. And if the people (and pooch) watching aren't enough, there's always a musician wailing over by the swings, a mime cavorting under the trees, a magician performing in the fountain basin. Some of the most awesome free-style Frisbee sailing and the baaadest skateboarding are served up for your amusement, the whole of the park's intricate choreography moving to the accompaniment of several dozen high-decibel ghetto boxes in an atmosphere of congenial chaos.

In May an art show spills out onto the adjoining streets. In June the headliners from the JVC Jazz Festival donate their time and tunes. And free classical concerts wind up the season in July and August.

No wonder the NYU students who live in the 1830s rowhouses to the north (formerly occupied by Henry James, Eleanor Roosevelt, and Edward Hopper) complain that they can't study. Who could study with the constant clamor from beyond Stanford White's 1865 arch? In fact, perhaps it's a mistake to suggest beginning your tour in the park—its incessant flow of scenes is so mesmerizing, you may never want to leave.

The park's rhythms are merely an overture to the symphony of sensation the Village waits to perform for your pleasure. Point your steps north up MacDougal

Street toward Eighth Street, a manic thoroughfare whose low prices reflect proportionate quality. If, however, you're in the market for a pair of off-the-wall shoes to scandalize the folks back home, you'll get just what you pay for. One exception is the **Capezio**'s you passed on your way up MacDougal (make sure to peep down picturesque but private MacDougal Alley). Capezio's has funky Italian- and Japanese-designed clothes for men and women, and employees are all off-hours dancers, so your salesperson is sure to be bopping with perfect turnout to the store's great music selections.

Turn right on Eighth Street and walk to Fifth Avenue for a backward glance at the park and a turn-of-the-head to the Washington Mews, vacated stables now housing NYU's foreign language students—there's certain to be the lilt of *français* or *italiano* floating through the air. Head up the avenue two blocks and turn west on Tenth Street, a street liberally laced with an eclectic selection of eateries: A waft of **Texarkana**'s babyback ribs sails over to the tofu and hijiki grazers at **Whole Wheat and Wild Berries.**

At Sixth Avenue and 9th Street (lying in wait to ensnare the unsuspecting gourmet) is the last word thereon, and that word is: **Balducci's.** On a Saturday afternoon the beautiful people are crammed in as tightly as the lobsters in the tank as you enter. But while the clientele can be as cantankerous as cramped crustaceans, the salespeople are very pleasant and will gladly let you sample a half-dozen cheeses or every pasta salad they sell till you're satisfied. Balducci's is a great picnic provider; they'll pack a lunch for you to enjoy alfresco as you continue your tour.

Across Sixth Avenue is a bizarre brick turreted affair, the **Jefferson Market Courthouse,** built in 1878, now a branch of the New York Public Library famous for its free film series Thursdays at 6 P.M. With classics from Cecil B. DeMille to Woody Allen, at these prices, it fills up fast, so come early. This is also the meeting place for many of the Greenwich Village walking tours, which run twice daily for two hours, hitting the historical and literary highlights. Times and locations change, so be sure to call in advance (675–3213).

On the far side of the library is Christopher Street, the center of New York's homosexual community, although the specifically gay bars and shops are a bit farther west toward the Hudson River. **Matt McGhee,** 18–22 Christopher St., is a toy store for discerning children and childlike grown-ups, and therefore is at its best around the holidays.

Past the triangular Northern Dispensary, still providing office space for doctors as it has since 1827, are the pair of parks that comprise Sheridan Square—a statue of the general stands in the northern one.

Across Seventh Avenue from Sheridan Square, West 4th Street extends to the right. Ready for a break? Surrender yourself to **Patisserie Lanciani** at 271 West 4th St. They serve a mean cappuccino, lighter-than-air pastries, and their cognac truffles are the finest in the city.

A left turn down 11th Street, powdered by pale pink blossoms in the spring, brings you from the streets of tranquility to one of the most cacophonous corners in Manhattan: At 401 Bleecker St. is the **Bird Jungle** whose feathered friends are permitted to run—or perch, or fly —wild and fancy free.

Across Bleecker is **Biography Bookshop,** a paperback and hardcover haven for the hard core, a place to find reads about folks from Princess Grace to Prince (Rogers Nelson).

A different assortment of scents greets you from 379 Bleecker where **Pierre Deux** proffers the *crème de la crème* of provincial France. In the back are cheerful florals and rich paisleys at $27 per 50-inch yard. The fabrics have been wrapped around picture frames, puffed into pillows, and fashioned into romantic frocks that fill the rest

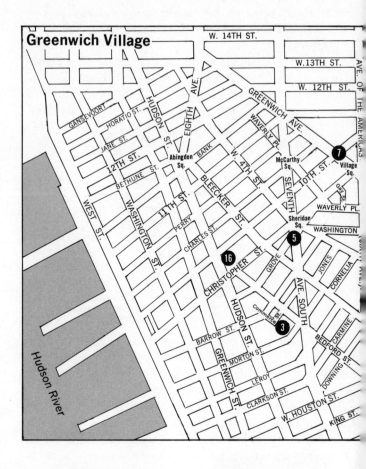

Points of Interest

1) Astor Place Theater
2) Bottom Line
3) Cherry Lane Theater
4) Circle in the Square Theater
5) Circle Repertory
6) Cooper Union
7) Jefferson Market Library
8) The New Museum/The New School (branch)
9) The New School for Social Research
10) New York University
11) Palladium
12) Players Theater
13) Provincetown Playhouse
14) Public Theater (Papp)
15) Sullivan St. Playhouse
16) Theater De Lys
17) Village Gate

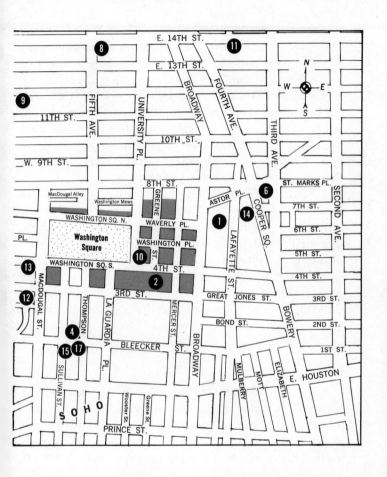

of the store. If all this fails to evoke an *ooo-la-la*, the second Pierre Deux down the block at No. 367 will surely strike you as *formidable.*

Turn right off Bleecker onto Grove Street. Behind the crisp curtains at No. 42 is the **Pink Teacup,** the only place in New York that serves up gen-u-ine ham hocks, pig's feet, and cheese grits. The corner of Grove and Bedford is punctuated by an 1830s Greek Revival wooden house, wisteria winding up its facade, backed by another wooden house, reconstructed after a fire, that once served as a stable. As Grove veers to the right, look in on the private square of houses, Grove Court, where O. Henry lived and worked for a time.

Sybaritic villagers bop down Barrow Street, a block south of Grove, to the Hudson River at Pier 42 in the summer for sipping, smooching, and sunsets over Jersey. If your Balducci's bag has miraculously remained intact this long, a riverside picnic with the island of Manhattan behind you and the continent of North America before you is a marvelous way to chase the day away. After the sun sets, however, the pier gets deserted and dicey fast.

Just beyond Bedford Street to the left is a red and white courtyard at the far end of which lies the formidable-looking door of **Chumley's,** at No. 86. (Look for it—there's no sign, neon or otherwise.) Easily the Village's coziest bar, Chumley's used to be a speakeasy and it still has the same air of secret fun that attracted John Dos Passos, John Steinbeck, and Ring Lardner. Chumley's is especially inviting on a cold winter's evening, when you can draw your chair up to the fire and wrap your paws around a hot rum toddy. You can still order a black and tan, and the bartender will pull you a half pint o' Guinness and a half o' Bass with narry a blink.

Sustained by Chumley's internally and externally warming spirits, you'll want to pay your respects at 75½ Bedford St. to speculate on how Edna St. Vincent Millay and John Barrymore both managed to squeeze their egos into New York's narrowest house. At different times, of course.

A left on Seventh Avenue will bring you to Bleecker Street again, this particular stretch of which is famous for its eye-popping, mouth-watering Italian provisioners. In the windows of **Ottomanelli's,** at No. 281, hang fresh hare, suckling pig, and an occasional pheasant. Several generations of **Zitos** at No. 259 have been baking New York's crispiest-outside, chewiest-inside loaves of Italian bread, both white and whole wheat. (It's the only bread Frank Sinatra eats when he's in town.) Another "best of" is **John's Pizzeria,** as the perpetual line around the block attests. In all weathers villagers and visitors queue up to sample pizza fresh from John's brick ovens. But John won't stand for nibblers—you can't buy just a slice for all the tortellini in Tuscany—eat a whole pie or eat elsewhere.

Thompson Street on either side of Bleecker offers a slew of diversions, one of which is guaranteed to stop you dead in your tracks. On the north side, at No. 230, is the **Chess Shop** where you can buy a game or just play one. The atmosphere is low key, so don't be shy about having a go even if you're not Bobby Fisher. Backgammon and books are also available. The **Village Comic Shop** is sure to make a drooler out of any DC devotee. **Nostalgia and All That Jazz** is the place to go for that Bix Beiderbecke record or the perfect still of Curly Howard you've hunted for everywhere. On the south side, at No. 169, **Modern Girls** caters to just that, with hats to die for, gold lamé bustiers, and outlandish jewelry you'd pay twice as much for if the shop hopped across Houston Street to Soho.

If you're of a pioneering spirit, head west to eat till it ouches at **Tortilla Flats,** 12th and Washington (Mexican—check out the mammoth margaritas); **The Gulf Coast,** 12th and West (Cajun—don't miss the crawfish); or **Florent,** Gansevoort and Washington (funky French —be sure to buss Florent on *both* cheeks). This trinity has

lured the uptown crowd to this picturesquely dubious
locale by following a formula best described as malt-shop
chic: slap up some fixtures from the local diner, serve up
some no-frills food, and crank up the jukebox—real loud.

After your meal, if you're still in the mood for slum-
ming with debs and celebs, you won't want to miss disco
night at **Bowlmor Lanes,** off Washington Square on University Place. It's a kick just to take an elevator up to the
third floor to *go bowling.*

If you prefer to let others work themselves into a
sweat for your entertainment, some of the best theater
Off-Broadway has to offer (at half what you'd pay on the
Great White Way) can be seen at the **Cherry Lane,
Minetta Lane, Circle in the Square, Circle Rep,** and
Provincetown Playhouse.

The **Lone Star Cafe** and the **Bottom Line** serve up
hot cuts of rock and roll; the **Village Gate, Blue Note,
Village Vanguard,** and **Seventh Avenue South** provide
cool licks of jazz. Most of these places sport a drink
minimum in addition to a hefty cover charge, so be aware
of the tariff in advance to insure that you're not washing
Dizzy Gillespie's or Tower of Power's dishes after the 2
A.M. set.

Nell's, on the south side of 14th Street, has become
a tradition even as it attempts to be a trend-setter. Host-
ess Nell Campbell (whom you can catch as "Little Nell"
in *The Rocky Horror Picture Show*) forsook the formulaic
cavernous disco genre and opened a small, intimate club
with comfy chairs for her pals like Sting and Bowie inside,
and a squad of insufferable doorkeepers outside, food
upstairs, dancing downstairs. Try to get in if you can—if
you care.

If you happen to have the good fortune to find yourself in town on Oct. 31 (and it's well worth a special trip),
the annual **Village Halloween Parade** gives vent to all
the suppressed desires of every zany for blocks around.
Drag queens get themselves up as Carmen Miranda or

Glinda the Good Witch or an entire Miss America pageant. Kids come as nurses or Darth Vadar or Chinese take-out or the IRT. Your favorite landmarks wind sinuously through the sidestreets and sashay down Fifth Avenue to the park: The Empire State and Chrysler buildings are always there, and the Statue of Liberty is now completely renovated.

SOHO AND TRIBECA

Soho is short for "South of Houston" (How-ston) and Tribeca stands for "Triangle Below Canal." Soho and Tribeca are largely responsible for the art, fashion, and mind set that epitomize the Downtown scene: When you're touring here, wear something asymmetrical or black, preferably both.

The spirit of the avant-garde is alive and kicking on these narrow, bricked streets with their cast-iron buildings. Pioneers in the cinematic, fine, and performance arts ply their trade here; only now they are paid quite handsomely for it, which is not at all a bad thing.

The one problem with the influx of big bucks into the avant-garde is that the pressure to produce fashionable (salable) work is tremendous. With all this money suddenly at stake, there is no place or patience for a young artist to be bad on his way to becoming good. The incredible forward motion of Soho and Tribeca steamrolls all but the strongest, staunchest artists in its way.

The same dynamic holds true for the restaurants and shops here; a kind of commercial Darwinism clears out the stragglers in short order. Should several months slip by between your visits, undoubtedly a new boutique will have popped up on West Broadway, or the place where you last stopped for espresso will have been replaced by a gallery for African textiles. Being at the cutting edge of style is no easy task. It takes all the running you can do to stay in the same place and not get booted out of business by the next person who knows exactly what New York will be wanting *tomorrow*.

This sense of running faster and wilder comes as soon as you set foot on West Broadway, which begins on the south side of Houston.

The **Vorpal Gallery,** at No. 465, is one of the best in the neighborhood, tending to favor non-eye-assaulting painters and sculptors. The gallery's employees are extremely knowledgeable and will be happy to discuss the artist and work you have your eye on. And if you can't afford a canvas, you can always console yourself with a postcard.

The **Circle Gallery,** at No. 468, is a study in contrast with the understated Vorpal, where the nasty subject of money is tacit. The Circle is more like a department store (albeit a Saks rather than a K-Mart) for art. Prices appear next to each picture; they feature a few pieces by many artists rather than vice versa; they sell posters, jewelry, even gift certificates.

Victoria Falls, at No. 451, sells antique clothing and their own uncanny remakes of vintage frocks, skirts, and blouses produced in limited editions from creamy silks and soft woolens. They also have luscious lingerie and crisp petticoats for the romantic, tired of seeing her latest Laura Ashley on everyone else.

420 (at that address) houses four of Soho's major galleries, enabling you to hop from floor to floor and from photo-realism to surrealism and beyond. **Leo Castelli** and **Sonnabend** show contemporary artists comfortable in the world's major collections. **Charles Cowles** features painting, sculpture, and photography of the great and soon-to-be so. **49th Parallel** is the Manhattan venue for important Canadian artists. Across the street at No. 417 is **Mary Boone's** place. She has been the undisputed high priestess of the city's art coven for years. It's always worth a look-in to see what her bunch is up to.

If you're looking for something a tad more conventional to spiff up the home, have a look-in at **Ad Hoc Softwares,** at No. 410, a treasure trove of the kind of high-tech tidbits this neighborhood has helped to make a national passion. The presentation is as modern-age as the merchandise: bowls are stacked according to color and size, lamps are lined up one by one by one: rhythm, order, utility.

Make a right on Spring Street and have a browse through the **Spring Street Book Shop,** where you can rub shoulders with the local longhairs. The store carries a long list of periodicals (from around the world) and literary journals. Take a turn around the sales tables at the back of the store to see if there's a special on any titles on your must-read list.

Turning left down Thompson Street you'll see **Tous Les Caleçons** which loosely translates as "All the Undies." The idea is not as outlandish as it seems: Think of how comfy your boxers are. Tous Les Caleçons sells pajama-inspired sportswear in pretty cotton prints and plaids, imported from Paris.

If you're planning to do some writing of your own, you can turn off Thompson to 510 Broome St. and pick up a hand-bound journal or hand-made letter papers at **80 Papers.** They also sell writers' supplies and vintage photographs of New York.

At the corner of Thompson and Watts is the **Manhattan Brewing Company,** a collegiate hangout, on the second floor of which they serve pints of gold ale, royal amber, porter, and brown ale made on the third floor. (See *Restaurants* chapter.)

Across West Broadway is the somewhat (though not much) more sedate **Broome Street Bar,** a favorite hang out of long standing that serves some of New York's best burgers.

Behind the wooden door with the fan of delicate wrought iron is **Touba Mbacke,** a gallery for African art, (496 Broome). Beautifully wrought sculpture which belie their spiritual progeny—Picasso, Klee, Matisse. They

also sell pottery baskets and jewelry for those a bit
squeamish about having a fertility goddess in their den.

Make a right, traveling down a couple of long blocks
on Mercer to No. 11 where you'll find the ever-intriguing
Museum of Holography, open Wednesdays–Sundays.
In a nutshell, holography is 3–D laser photography
whose image and colors change as you change your position before the hologram. The museum proffers a permanent installation and a film explaining the technology
and tracing the history of holography. It also displays
rotating exhibits of various artists who are creating
"painting" and "sculpture" using holograms and other
media of light and illusion. The gift shop sells holograms
for your home or wardrobe.

Across from the museum is Howard Street, which
will lead you to Broadway, where you turn left. Your
ultimate destination is several blocks up, the **New Museum,** at No. 583, but as you're making your way north-
ward, the bargain hunter in you will begin to rear its ugly
head as you canvass the army surplus and odd-lot stores
whose wares range from funk to punk to junk. Lots of
Soho's in-the-knows divide their sartorial business between West Broadway and just plain Broadway. You'll
have to work your way through piles of junk and packs
of Downtowners, but there are definitely treasures to be
sniffed out at the lowest of low prices. Some happy hunting grounds are **Street Life,** at No. 470, and **Canal Jean
Co.,** at No.504.

The **New Museum,** between Prince and Houston
streets, is a mere babe, founded in 1977, and features
works that are no older than itself. The curators have an
uncanny ability to unearth and celebrate developing artists before the uptown galleries get their hands on them.
This is also one of the few museums that have a sense of
humor. Its exhibits run from deadly serious to downright
hilarious; open Wednesdays–Sundays, from noon to the
evening.

Backtrack half a block down Broadway to Prince Street. Just in from the corner on the west side of Mercer Street is **A Photographer's Place,** which is as much like a museum as a commercial shop. In cases and stacked on shelves in front are antique cameras and equipment. And to help you take better pictures, there is a comprehensive selection of photography books, new and out of print, and back issues of popular photography magazines.

If you take your libations just as seriously, some intense pleasantness awaits at **Fanelli**'s behind the cut-glass double doors next door at 94 Prince St. A beautiful tile floor supports the richly carved darkwood bar and the locals who water themselves at this oasis of old New York in the midst of nouveau chic Soho. This welcome retreat, with its friendly tapsters and tapees is a great place to pause and catch a quarter of the game on an autumn afternoon.

Thus braced, continue down Prince to Nos. 116 and 118, where **Agnès b.** and **Agnès b. Homme,** respectively, specialize in clothing of quiet, uncomplicated tailoring that lends a look of subtle sophistication. The prices are far from low, but check out the sale sections in back, for end-of-season deals.

Across Prince at No. 121 is **Dean and De Luca;** a heady waft of coffee envelopes you as you open the door. Greeting you as you enter is a profusion of near-perfect fresh vegetables and herbs, kept misted and glistening. At the rear of the store is a cornucopia of cookware whose quality reflects that of the edibles up front. These include black truffles just emigrated from Umbria, Italy, at $30 per ounce; pheasant and quail, stuffed with currants, wrapped in bacon and ready to roast; reprehensibly rich cassis mousse; and apple calvados cake. D&D has catalogue, will ship; so if you can't resist, you needn't.

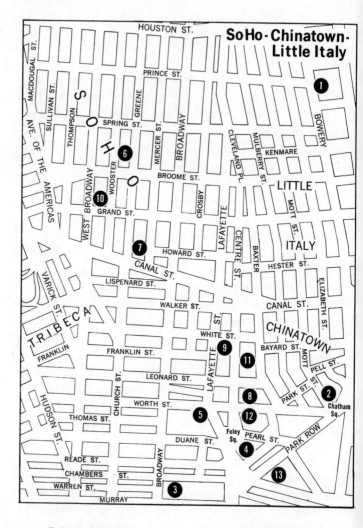

Points of Interest

1) Bowery Mission
2) Chinese Museum
3) City Hall
4) Federal Court
5) Federal Office Building
6) Museum of Colored Glass & Light
7) Museum of Holography
8) N.Y. State Office Building
9) N.Y. State Supreme Court
10) Performing Garage
11) Criminal Court
12) N.Y. County Court
13) Police Headquarters

But if you can't wait for the victuals to arrive on your doorstep back home, **Food,** at the corner of Prince and Wooster, will provide you with noshables you can enjoy on the spot. Don't let the generic name fool you; their menu is anything but the same old thing. Food's rich soups, quixotic combo sandwiches and mammoth slices of homemade desserts have made the place popular, so if you arrive at lunchtime be prepared to wait in line.

Down Wooster Street are a pair of new-wave haberdashers whose architecturally inspired clothing should be sold with a blueprint to help you figure out where the arms go. **Parachute,** at No. 121, has fashions that look Japanese but are really designed by Harry Parnass and Nicole Pelly. Check out the sales racks and the magazines. **Comme Des Garçons,** at No. 116, sounds French but is really Japanese. Their press says: "Unconfined by tradition or custom or geography. The strongest idea around." Strongest perhaps, strangest possibly; it's always wise to do a little reconnaissance in order to prepare yourself for what's coming next.

Turn right on Spring Street, and beyond the bars and boutiques you'll again pick up West Broadway; turn left and head south several blocks to No. 307, where **Sohozat** hovers several centimeters above the horizons of reality. It calls itself a space-age variety store and sells clothes and comics, gadgets and stickers, books and magazines that will move your consciousness into the 21st century.

Crossing Canal Street, you're leaving Soho and entering Tribeca. Where Soho can be complacent, Tribeca tries harder, and you'll have to do the same to scout out the various haunts scattered fewer and farther between here. But the legwork is worth it; prices and haughtiness are generally at a lower level than above Canal Street.

If you're starting to slow down a bit, turn left onto Walker, cross Church to get revved up at **Exterminator Chili** on the northeast corner. Each day the chef fires up four specials: Residential—mild; Commercial—hot; Industrial—infernal; and Agricultural—vegetarian. Bring your own beers to douse the flames. Down Church, make a right onto White Street. At No. 17 is the **Alternative Museum,** a ground-floor loft space (is that a contradiction?) featuring the kind of things you'd expect to see in such a place in this neighborhood. It is an eclectic view of what is going on in the arts on these streets. Pick up a calendar of film and music events inside the front door. Open Tuesday–Saturday.

Walk past the **Odeon** at 145 West Broadway, made famous by Jay McInerney's yuppy odyssey, *Bright Lights, Big City,* to **Ice Maker** at No. 123. Andy Tse cut his teeth buying for stores in Soho and has pumped that fashion savvy into this collection of casual craziness from Denmark, Japan, Scotland, Hong Kong—wherever in the world he finds "modern clothes with clean lines, that have a classical and cultural background."

As you make a right on Chambers Street and walk west, there is a great view of the river, soon to be constructed over, so enjoy it while you can. At 153 Chambers is **Cheeses of All Nations.** Connoisseurs who know good cheese and great bargains when they sniff them come from boroughs around to shop here. Specials are plastered all over the wall, with few exceeding $4 a pound.

Walk west to Greenwich then cut back east past the little park on Duane to Hudson, where you'll make a left in front of the 1930s polychrome brick Western Union Building. **Puffy's Tavern** is a homey haunt, at 81 Hudson, but the real news is the **Sporting Club,** at No. 99. This huge fun house for sports fans runs athletic events continuously on six monitors and a ten-foot screen next to the bar. (See *Restaurants* chapter.) The crowd ambles up from Wall Street for happy hour, 4–7, with 25-cent oysters and clams.

If you don't find Monday Night Football particularly mind-expanding, evenings in these parts offer a chance to see the performing arts side of the avant-garde. At 33 Wooster is the **Performing Garage,** a long-time proponent of experimental theater, music, and dance. Under the direction of Elizabeth LeComte, the Garage has produced many ground-breaking theatrics and many famous alumni—Oscar nominee Willem DaFoe and raconteur Spalding Gray, among others. The **Film Forum,** on Watts Street, showcases a choice collection of the world's great, if not always commercial, cinema.

If you prefer to be a part of the moving pictures, tropical scenes are shot on the dance floors of **SOB's** (Sounds of Brazil), West Houston and Varick; and the **Reggae Lounge,** 285 West Broadway. Check the *Village Voice* for who's playing. You may also want to check out what's cooking at the **Ear Inn,** a delightful little dive on Spring Street between 11th and 12th. They might be featuring live music or readings—and if not, the jukebox is great and the food is cheap.

NOHO AND EAST VILLAGE

Noho (North of Houston) and the East Village would not have appeared in any guidebook five years ago. Up from the rubble, out of the tenements has been created (and some say, already exploited and ruined) an artists' colony, a testing ground for ideas far from the mainstream. The names of East Village-based artists who've made good form a Who's Who of contemporary creativity: Keith Haring, Ann Magnuson, Talking Heads, Kenny Scharf, Laurie Anderson.

This is the place to come for the spectacle of pierced noses and mohawks on the wanest people imaginable, whose ashenness is further accentuated by their exclusively black toilettes. While experiencing continued gentrification, the neighborhood still has maintained certain standards of grit and tawdriness. If it looks like a tough place, that's because it is.

The people who live and play here (excluding the large Ukrainian and Hispanic populations) don't tend to have hours in sync with the rest of the world. People don't start packing the clubs till way past midnight, go wild till dawn, then crash till midafternoon when they arise again for the next evening's indiscretions. You'll have to adapt to the East Village clock. Many galleries are closed Mondays and Tuesdays; the balance of the week, things will open around noon and stay open into the evening.

You'll want to begin your tour looking right. **Astor Place Haircutters** is the place to go for a tease or a buzz or a green and pink rinse. The $5 price has climbed to $8 for men, $10 for women, but the line still stretches out the door on weekends.

Now you'll need some Noho threads to match your new "do," and down Broadway you'll find a parade of new and vintage clothing stores that keep the neighborhood properly retro. **Zoot,** at No. 734, hands out good buttons, so stop there. The huge windows fronting **Unique** allow you to watch people painting or making spin-art T- and sweatshirts. But don't just stand there gawking, it's great fun to get inside and make your own. **Basic Basic** No. 710, has fashions that are a bit more European and upscale, yet still at basic prices. The **Antique Boutique** No. 714, is the sartorial equivalent of central casting for NYU—no matter what one looks like when one enters, everyone who leaves does so clothed as the archetypical Downtown type.

On West 4th Street you'll see **Tower Records,** from which everyone is emerging with their red and yellow bags. Skip it and save your record-buying bucks for **J&R Records** downtown, or better, walk down 4th Street to **Tower's Classical** annex, a *much* better deal.

South on Lafayette Street, turn left onto Great Jones where, more typical of the neighborhood, is the **Great Jones Café** at the corner of Bowery. The door is blue and the exterior is orange (to remind you of your youth at

Howard Johnson's). The inside is smoky and not too self-consciously artsy. Happy hour is 4–6.

Cross Bowery and walk up in the direction of the large red building (Cooper Union). You might want to make a quick dash down Fourth Street to see what's doing at the **Truck and Warehouse Theater,** at No. 79 or at **LaMaMa ETC.,** at No. 66. The latter, especially, presents fine new-wave theater and dance. If *Ping Chong* is playing, don't miss it.

Another detour off Bowery is down Seventh Street where you'll find, as undoubtedly your fathers did before you, **McSorley's Ale House,** at No. 15. McSorley's light and dark ales are served in mugs; buy them by twos, since the portions are small and it's a better deal at $1.25 for the pair. Weekend nights college students queue up for hours to get in, so try to stop by late in the afternoon instead.

Your ultimate destination is St. Marks Place (one block north of Seventh). You'll spot a nasty mural which says "Gringo" slapped up on the outside of a building, so you'll know you're there. St. Marks embodies the commercialization of the trends that originated in the East Village and made it famous: used clothes, scrappy street merchants, ethnic food, cacophonous music.

Sounds, up the steps at No. 20, has a good selection of new and used records, especially hard-to-find reggae and punk. The **St. Marks Bookshop,** at No. 13, is good for literary journals, and books and periodicals to the left of center. **Dojos** is populated by New Yorkers from all over town (there may be a line) because the food is cheap and good and the outdoor cafe is great for street-watching.

Turn right at Second Avenue. **Freebeing Records** is at No. 129, with a substantial supply of new wave, domestic and imported. You'll remember **Love Saves the Day,** at No. 119, as the shop where Madonna unloaded her fateful jacket in *Desperately Seeking Susan.* Across Seventh

Street at No. 117 is the **Kiev,** open 24 hours for very inexpensive Ukrainian vittles served to you, more often than not, by young ladies just off the boat. Even better for this type of cooking is **Vaselkas,** at 122 Second Ave.

Continue down Second and make a left onto Sixth Street or "Little Bombay" as it's sometimes called in reference to the string of Indian restaurants along its south side. Most of them are BYOB, but will still honor your credit card. The best is generally agreed to be **Mitali** at No. 334, (which, perhaps not coincidentally, does have a liquor license), but if the line is long there, the difference between the various curries on the block is not very great.

In between the Indians are two other ethnic representatives: **Back from Guatemala,** at No. 304, has bright-colored sweaters, scarves, masks, and jewelry. **Yuzen,** at No. 318, sells beautifully made vintage and new kimonos. Prices range from $70 to $125 on up for the antiques which, if you don't care to hang on yourself, will look fantastic hung on your wall.

Continue on Sixth Street, turning left on First Avenue and right on St. Marks toward **Tompkins Square Park**, which is to the East Village (in a twisted way) what Washington Square Park is to the West Village. Tompkins Square is a bit bedraggled and not so supercharged as its western counterpart, but this area is more grungy and low key, so the park merely reflects the pervasive lack of concern with keeping up conventional appearances.

The numbered avenues end here in Alphabet Land, so your next right will be on Avenue A, for which is named a sushi bar just below Seventh Street. The fish is very fresh, the art shows provocative, the waitresses emaciated.

At 101 Avenue A is the Pyramid Club, still one of the best joints going, but more on that later. Get a glance at the facade when it's not obscured by darkness or a crowd. Turn left down Sixth Street then left again on Avenue B.

The bar on the corner of Seventh and B has no name on the outside, but you'll recognize the interior from *The Verdict,* part of which was filmed here (not in Boston). Drinks are cheap and the atmosphere surprisingly friendly for these parts.

Walk along the perimeter of the park, turning left on 10th Street and right again on Avenue A, where you'll spot **Gracie Mansion** (named for a person, not named for the mayor's place), at No. 167, and **Hal Bromm,** at No. 170, two of the more visible galleries in the area. Turn left on 11th, then left again on First to **DiRobertis** (No. 176), a pastry and coffee spot since 1904. It's heaven on earth for late-night munchies, open till 1 A.M. on weekends. As John DiRobertis says, baking every day "is not my work, it's my pastime." Try the mocha peaks or the calzones, fresh lemon ice in the summer, steamed milk flavored with almond in the winter.

The blocks between Second Avenue and Avenue A, and from 4th to 12th streets are East Village Gallery country. It's impossible to suggest one over another because the type and quality of the work depends on the artist being shown and, of course, on the taste of the viewer. This is a good point in the tour to allow yourself an hour or several to serpentine through these streets, stopping at whatever window catches your eye. The tour resumes at 10th Street and Second Avenue, so get yourself back there when you've OD'd on art.

At the northwest corner of Second and 10th is **St. Marks in the Bouwerie,** a church standing since 1799 despite recent attempts to purchase the property and tear it down. Take 10th Street across several blocks to Broadway, at the corner of which is another beautiful building, **Grace Church.** Turn right and north to the corner of 12th Street. At 828 Broadway is the **Strand Book Store,** miles of new and used volumes packed in at low prices. Across the street is **Forbidden Planet,** which always has the coolest window displays of its sci-fi merchandise. They stock a full line of books, masks, models, and toys to assist you in anticipating what the future has in store.

There is an endless variety of clubs in this neighborhood, from the large and luxurious to the small and sleazy. **CBGB's** has nurtured many growing talents, from Lou Reed to the Ramones. The atmosphere is close and grimy, but it's still possible to catch stars on the rise. **The Saint** has been a strictly gay stronghold for all its life until now—Friday has been designated as "straight night." The place is large and also something of a local standard, so go on whichever night suits you sexually.

The aforementioned **Pyramid Club** is best during the week late at night when the NYU crowd is in abeyance. The drag queens dance go-go on the bar, though it's not necessarily a gay club—music, melodrama, and much more are in the back room. **The World,** which has been around just over a year (a good record in this neighborhood), is new-wavey and slam-dancey. Go late and stay till early.

The glitz clubs here are the **Ritz** and the **Palladium.** Although the acoustics are disappointing, the Ritz manages year after year to get the best live acts around before everyone else. For example, U2, Sting, the Eurhythmics, and Husker Du played here to the precocious and appreciative bunch of students, stockbrokers, and studio artists that comprise the Ritz's clientele. The Palladium is another brainstorm of Studio 54 founders. The cover is $20 on weekends (plus $1.25 to check your coat, $4 to drink a beer). Upstairs behind the balcony seats is the Mike Todd Room (sometimes private), which is a pleasant, relatively sane place to sit one out. Definitely not to miss are the downstairs lounges, decorated by various Downtown art scene fixtures. The Palladium peaks between 1 and 3 A.M., so try to come a little early to see everything.

Downtown

In 1792 under a spreading butternut tree several forward-looking Yanks sat down with their tankards and birthed the New York Stock Exchange. Will the world ever be the same?

Look, you want excitement? You want high rolling? You don't have to hop a Greyhound to Atlantic City. The fastest, most ferocious game east of the Mississippi is run by the Wall Street crapshooters, three-piece suiters. They're very serious about their game, their gambles. Although people don't defenestrate anymore, they do go quietly mad.

There's something in the air down here. The buildings are very tall, built to impress; the streets are narrow. The sun shines on the sidewalk for maybe five minutes in August. It's easy to dismiss the game of finance as capitalism run amok and Downtown as its sunless citadel. But the people here who really do well, who make the megabucks, are generally not avaricious twerps, calculator in one hand, ticker tape in one hand, telephone in one hand, secretary's tush in one hand.

The people on the Street (Wall is the only street in town whose first name is optional) who consistently make the right calls have smarts, of course, but they also have *imagination.* And they love their work probably more than they love their wages. Collar one of the gray-flannel guys or gals you see scampering about; he or she will talk to you of nothing but the Market.

It's fitting to start the day at the World Trade Center: two tall, steely skyscrapers which simply exude power. At One WTC is **Windows on the World,** a restaurant, and the **Hors D'Oeuverie,** a bar. Both have a 107-story view. (See *Restaurants* chapter.) Should you not feel like dining and/or spending, you can enjoy much the same view from the observation deck on the 107th floor or outside on the roof (110 floors) of Two WTC for $2.95, 9:30–9:30, seven days a week.

As you leave Two WTC there is a **TKTS** outlet, with

Broadway on sale for half price, situated to the left of the Joan Miró tapestry on the mezzanine level. The lines are generally much shorter than at the TKTS in Times Square.

As you leave the building, stop in at the green market on Church Street (Tuesdays and Thursdays) for some cider and a doughnut, and have a glance upward at the lacy traceries of the Woolworth Building, capped in green to your left, with St. Paul's Chapel in the foreground. Walk toward St. Paul's, down Fulton Street, and turn right on Broadway. Things are pretty honky-tonk down here at street level until you come to the intersection of Broadway and Wall Street, where stands **Trinity Church,** protected from encroaching mercenariness by its green churchyard, final resting place of Alexander Hamilton and Robert Fulton, among others. The building you see was built in 1846, after fires destroyed its predecessors. There are chapel and churchyard tours daily at 2, and free concerts on Tuesdays at 12:45 P.M. —pick up a program to the right inside the finely detailed bronze doors.

Continue south down Broadway to Bowling Green and the **Custom House** (1907), whose history is related on a kiosk erected in the shape of the building. To the right is Battery Park. If you take a path sharp to the right, you'll come upon a gray building with crimson trim, parked outside of which are some of the city's fireboats. Along the water is an esplanade with coin-operated binoculars at strategic intervals. You might want to settle on the steps in front of the fierce stone eagle (a World War II memorial) and have a look at the Statue of Liberty and Ellis Island, past which and through which your ancestors might have come.

It's easy, with the insularity of the concrete canyons, to forget that the city's an island. Here at its prow the scent of the wind and the sound of the water are reminders that Manhattan's greatness was based initially on its supremacy as a port. You can get out on the water to see the **Statue of Liberty** or Staten Island (every 15 minutes Monday–Friday, every half hour on weekends; round-trip fare, 25 cents), from the ferry depots at the park. Statue tickets ($3.25 round-trip) can be purchased inside the circular Castle Clinton for ferries departing every half hour 10 A.M.–5 P.M. Another $1 will be collected at the statue's entrance.

Cross Peter Minuit Plaza, across from the ferry depots, toward the low brick buildings, turning right on State Street then left on Broad Street to **Fraunces Tavern.** Upstairs is a museum run by the Sons of the Revolution commemorating George Washington's farewell to his officers here in 1783. Downstairs it's still doing what it does best—serving up rib-sticking American food, especially inviting in winter when they've got the fireplaces going.

Circumambulate 85 Broad St., the large brown affair across from Fraunces Tavern, ringed by specialty shops in restored 19th century buildings.

Returning to Broad Street, continue to No. 20, on your left, where on the third floor is the Visitors Center of the **New York Stock Exchange.** There are half-hour self-guided tours from 9:30 A.M. to 3:30 P.M. Electronic question-and-answer consoles on the walls help you tell the difference between common and preferred, bulls and bears, and other beasties of the Street's lingo.

You can bypass the media presentation and make a beeline for the visitors gallery above the floor of the Exchange—the most fascinating fishbowl extant. Just seeing the frantic scurryings of the brokers and the specialists, and watching the ticker tape zoom by will have your palms itching to play the Market more than any tired filmloop ever could. You've seen the scene a million times on TV, but to be there in person, hearing the whoops and watching ecstatic eruptions of paper, is positively riveting.

After you've made a call to your broker and taken out a second mortgage to snap up 10,000 shares of Amalgamated Sump Pump, walk up to Federal Hall at Wall Street, open 9 A.M. to 5 P.M. Monday–Friday. You'll recognize the building, it's the one down whose steps the bull clatters and the lion pads in all those commercials. There are noontime concerts here on Wednesdays and colonial folk music daily at 12, 1, 2, and 4.

Turn right down Wall and up Williams, then up the stairs to your left on Pine Street, where you'll come upon the Chase Manhattan Plaza (actual open space in this cramped part of town), in the midst of which is a large black and white sculpture, *Group of Four Trees* by Jean Dubuffet. At least you can see the sky here and plenty of future magnates taking the air and worrying about their careers at lunchtime.

Leave the plaza to the right as you face the statue and the Chase building. Go onto William Street, which runs into Louise Nevelson Plaza, containing a grouping of the artist's sculptures. Turn right down Maiden Lane, left on Water Street.

A couple of blocks up is **South Street Seaport.** Spot the museum if you can, it's there somewhere. Admission is $4 to go aboard the vessels on Piers 15 and 16 and into some restored buildings. Around the museum the Rouse Corporation has built one of its signature waterfront restorations. The plan is essentially the same as in all Rouse enterprises: a warehouseful of stores and restaurants. It's remarkable what homogeneity can be achieved if you put your mind to it.

Reservations aside, the Seaport provides a much-needed reason for touring this area. When New Yorkers yearn for a taste of the suburbs, they come here on weekends, when the place is jammed with bridge and tunnel people from across the various rivers. Weekday afternoons it's quite pleasant, much less crowded. Most evenings the young lions of Wall Street congregate at the various bars and drink themselves silly.

If you prefer to rub shoulders with people from all over, the area is especially electric on the Fourth of July, with street theater, musicians, and fireworks. The best jazz in town is down on the pier, where you can sit below

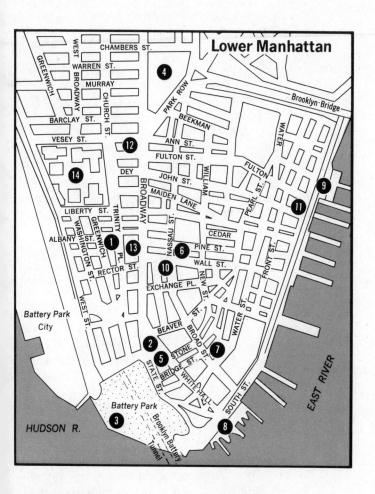

Lower Manhattan

Points of Interest

1) American Stock Exchange
2) Bowling Green
3) Castle Clinton Nat. Monument
4) City Hall
5) Customs House
6) Federal Hall Memorial
7) Fraunces Tavern
8) Ferry to Staten Island
9) Fulton Fish Market
10) N.Y. Stock Exchange
11) South Street Seaport
12) St. Paul's Chapel
13) Trinity Church
14) World Trade Center

the masts, the lights of Lower Manhattan twinkling on behind you on a summer's evening. If you're itching to leave dry land, you can sail out on the *Pioneer* or steam out on the *Andrew Fletcher*, which leave from the seaport. Reservations are necessary: Pioneer, 669–9424; Andrew Fletcher, 406–3434. In the good-weather months there are lunch cruises departing daily at 11:30, jazz brunch cruises on weekends, and evening jazz cruises. Check the information booth on Front and Fulton for schedules.

Whether aboard boat or on land in the area, take time to admire one of New York's true wonders—the **Brooklyn Bridge.** Pictures don't do it justice, neither do words, though countless writers have sung its praises. Enjoy it from afar, then walk across its roaring, soaring span to catch the breeze and the Statue of Liberty in the harbor at sunset.

For a bit of authenticity you might want to forsake the food halls and eat at **Sweets,** upstairs at 2 Fulton St. (344–9186), open 11:30 A.M.–8:30 P.M. weekdays; closed weekends because the fresh Fulton Market fish they insist on is not delivered Saturday and Sunday. Less expensive is **Sloppy Louie's,** which, along with its surroundings, has had a face-lift but still retains much of its old charm. If you really want to see (and smell) what the neighborhood was really all about, walk up South Street to the fish markets under the FDR Drive.

When you've had enough Seaport, turn back up Fulton Street, right on Nassau Street (a pedestrian mall), then left on little Ann Street where you'll spot the **Mendoza Book Company,** upstairs at No. 15, an old book store that looks and smells just right.

Continue up Ann Street to Park Row, to your right and upstairs at No. 23. Here is **J and R Music World,** where prices and selection are by far the best in town, so grab an armload. There is also a classical and jazz outlet up the street.

Across from Park Row are the somewhat less harmonious seats of government: **City Hall,** the ornate pale building at the head of City Hall Park, and the court and government buildings looming behind.

From here you have several choices of destination: bargain hunting on the Lower East Side or window-shopping and dining in Chinatown or Little Italy.

The shopping on the Lower East Side centers on Orchard Street from Grand to Houston. At first glance, the street looks like total trash, but under the tackiness are some serious French and Italian fashions at low, low prices. Most places take plastic, so you can spend with wild abandon and clear conscience.

Things are open until three hours before sundown on Friday; closed Saturdays for the Sabbath. When the shops reopen on Sunday, pandemonium ensues. Madelyn, who works at **Chez Aby** (79 Orchard), advises the out-of-towner against coming on Sundays. "You won't be able to get the attention you want; it's full of people haggling with the salespeople or fighting over the last one of an item." Prices can be one-third of what you'd pay for the same outfit in a Soho boutique, and many shopkeepers can be talked down in price, if you've the stamina.

Mott Street is the main drag in Chinatown for dim sum and knickknacks. Traffic jams are perpetual in these tiny, winding streets, with trucks unloading vegetables and fish you've never seen or smelled or tasted before. The hustle is underscored by the constant clickety-clack of Cantonese. Things can get uproariously cutesy here—Chemical Bank and telephone booths shaped like pagodas.

Everyone may not agree on the best food in Chinatown, but a good way to judge what's what is to peek in several restaurants and find the one with the highest percentage of Chinese customers—the locals of course know the best food and the best value.

Little Italy interlaces with Chinatown in one of

NYC's most peculiar ethnic juxtapositionings. The restaurants range from fine and fancy to fine and folksy. Things get particularly out of hand during the San Gennaro festival in September. It's colorful and animated, but has that certain undertone of dinge that makes most carnivals a little depressing.

Both Chinatown and Little Italy are improved by nightfall (although you get more local color during the day); the limos slip in and out and minks bob among the masses. Most fun is to have dinner one place, then find an outdoor café and imbibe liberal doses of cappuccino, pastry, and the scene.

CENTRAL PARK AND BEYOND

After all the running around you've been doing, it's possible that the last thing you want to hear about is further possibilities in and out of Manhattan. But some are too fine to be denied, so we're duty-bound to apprise you of all the rest there is to do.

Perhaps you've noticed that Central Park has hardly been mentioned. That's mostly because the park doesn't fit into the Upper East or West sides, but deserves its own space.

Weekends are sublime in the park. Visit the Great Lawn to watch the Uptown girls and boys applying themselves to the business of softball, football, and soccer. In the summer the Great Lawn is transformed by Calliope herself when the **New York Philharmonic** and the **Metropolitan Opera** give free concerts and New Yorkers spread their picnics—complete with pâté, chèvre, champagne, and candelabras (no kidding)—as far as the eye can see. Other fun summerfare is the New York Shakespeare Festival's productions at the **Delacorte Theater,** on the southwest corner of the Great Lawn. Although admission is free, you must stand in a very long line for tickets handed out at 6 P.M., so plan to arrive by late afternoon.

Rollerskating is at its most elaborate by the volleyball courts just south of the 72nd Street crossover. Ice-skating is at the rink off 110th Street and, thanks to Donald Trump, at the refurbished Wollman Rink. The **Carousel** just south of the Sheep Meadow is a blissful spin for children of all ages.

Biking is always fun (although serious racers tend to favor Brooklyn's less-crowded Prospect Park). You can rent bikes from various shops along the avenues bordering the park. Check the Yellow Pages for a convenient location. One of the nicest runs in town is the track around the reservoir (between 86th and 96th streets). For the serious runner, the New York City Marathon is run the third Sunday in October. If you prefer another animal to supply the power, Claremont Stables on West 79th Street will supply you with a mount at hourly rates (724–5100).

The zoo in Central Park is now being renovated, so if you're into fauna, much better is the **Bronx Zoo** (220–5100). It's spacious and has a large selection of beasts to observe as you safari through their habitat by train, monorail, or cable car.

While you're in the neighborhood, just north of the zoo is the **New York Botanical Garden,** most spectacular in spring, but the green is kept up all year round in its 11 greenhouses. To find out what's blooming, call 220–8777.

Also in the northern regions (this time still in Manhattan proper) is the **Cloisters,** overlooking the Hudson. The structure was brought over piece by piece and reconstructed from twelfth- and thirteenth-century buildings from France. It houses some of the Metropolitan Museum's vast medieval collection, including the detailed Unicorn Tapestries. A picnic in the park and a

stroll through the museum are a perfect afternoon's be-
guilement. At the end of September is a Renaissance
Festival, complete with wenches and jousting. At Christmas there are music programs. To ascertaineth what
transpireth, call 923–7000.

Sports fans, New York's roster will have you salivat-
ing if not dribbling or seeing doubles. There are at least
two of everything: **basketball**—the Nets and the Knicks;
baseball—the Mets and the Yankees; **football**—the Jets
and the Giants; and **hockey**—the Rangers, Islanders, and
Devils. The Knicks and Rangers (both 564–4400) shoot
and skate at Madison Square Garden. The Jets (421–
6600) and Giants (201–935–8222) and Devils (201–935–
6050) score safeties and kick-saves at the Meadowlands
in New Jersey. The Nets and Islanders (both 516–794–
9100) slam-dunk and slapshoot at the Nassau Coliseum
on Long Island. The Mets (718–507–8499) and Yankees
(293–6000) swat and steal at Shea Stadium in Queens
and Yankee Stadium in the Bronx, respectively. The **U.S.
Tennis Open** holds court at Flushing Meadow, Queens,
in early September.

Hotels

By Nancy B. Clarke

Most of the Big Apple's hotels are in the Midtown area. They range in style from old-world opulent to high-tech modern. Some have pool and sauna; others are the simple, no-frills type. Price? They're usually not cheap. But you *can* find accommodations for $100 a night for two persons. Our price reflects the cost of a standard double or twin-bedded room for two. Don't forget to add the 8 ¼ percent New York City sales tax and, maybe, an occupancy tax of $2 per night.

Even though there are more than 300,000 hotel rooms in New York City, it's always best to have a reservation. Major conventions, fashion buyers' weeks, and other special events make your chances of getting a last-minute lodging slim.

Be sure to check out special weekend packages. They're available at most hotels. These reduced weekend rates—when hotels are not filled with visiting business people—often will include tickets to a Broadway show, complimentary Sunday brunch, a free tour, or even a welcoming bottle of champagne. Also, remember to consider the proximity of your hotel to the location where you'll want to be spending most of your time. Frequent cab rides are costly, and public transportation can be time-consuming.

Our list of hotels is a sampling—a *select* sampling—of New York's extensive choice of lodgings. The criteria we've used are quality of service, location, and general ambience and style. Hotels are busy all year round, for New York is a year-round city; but September through November is their busiest time.

Besides listing the super deluxe hotels, we've listed some smaller, more modest (for New York, that is) establishments. These places have a special character, atmosphere, or location that will appeal to a discerning but not necessarily extravagant traveler.

Believe it or not, the English custom of afternoon tea is replacing the drink date and becoming increasingly popular at some of New York's finer hotels. Take a respite from shopping and sightseeing for tea at one of the grand hotels that really know how to serve it: Among the best are the Waldorf-Astoria, Carlyle, Plaza, Mayfair Regent, the Helmsley Palace, and the American Stanhope.

Most hotels accept all major credit cards. A few, however, prefer not to accept certain cards; these are indicated in our listing. Abbreviations for credit cards are: A, American Express; D, Diners Club; M, MasterCard; and V, Visa.

MIDTOWN

Though the **Algonquin** opened almost 90 years ago, today's comforts abound. This world-famous hotel, at 59 West 44th St. 10036 (840–6800), is noted for its civilized atmosphere and traditional hospitality to actors and writers. Rooms are cozy, quiet, with Early American decor. A sense of security here has made the Algonquin a favorite with businesswomen traveling alone. It is a perennial

favorite with English visitors, too, especially those in-
volved in the arts. The Algonquin was the setting for the
famous literary Round Table in the 1920s.

Nowadays, there is cabaret entertainment nightly in
the Oak Room; and the Edwardian Rose Room is a popular after-theater stop for its elegant buffet, which is available until 1 A.M. Drinks are served in the old-world lobby,
a friendly, oak-paneled, homey meeting place. The
miniscule Blue Bar, replete with James Thurber sketches,
is to the right of the entrance. A room at the Algonquin
is a real bargain at $118.

The **Carlyle,** Madison Ave. at 76th St. 10021 (744–
1600). The quiet elegance and attention to detail evident
throughout the Carlyle make a stay here unforgettable.
Each of the 175 rooms in this superdeluxe establishment
is distinct. Each has a Jacuzzi, fridge, terry cloth robes,
stereo, and VCR.

Pianist par excellence Bobby Short performs in the
Cafe Carlyle most nights. The Cafe serves a buffet luncheon during the day. Singer Barbara Carroll holds forth
at Bemelman's Bar, and the charming Carlyle Restaurant
serves classic continental cuisine. If you're ready to
splurge, or have just won the lottery, go for the 33rd-
floor suite. It has an unsurpassed view and comes with a
baby grand piano. Rate: $750. The rate for a standard
double room begins at $220.

Doral Park Avenue, 70 Park Ave., at 38th St. 10016
(687–7050). A relaxing oasis moments away from the
42nd Street hubbub. Gracious, multilingual staff. Huge
crystal chandelier and marble lobby add to a congenial,
warm ambience. The sidewalk cafe is a nice cooling-off
place during summer months. No room service after 10
P.M., but each room has a refrigerator, and some have
efficiency kitchens. Rates: from $168.

Only half of the **Dorset's** 431 rooms are available for
guests. The rest are rented on a permanent basis. This
quiet, independently owned hotel, located at 30 West

54th St., near Fifth Ave., 10019 (247–7300) has comfortable, Early American decor and some original art deco murals in its dining room, the Dorset Room. TV newsmen from nearby ABC and NBC are partial to the luncheon scene. The hotel's long suits are dignity and attention to detail. Rates: $155. No M or V.

Drake, 440 Park Ave., at 56th St., 10022 (421–0900). This gracious, 640-room hotel, in one of the most fashionable sections of town, is owned by Swissotel, and the Swiss tradition of gracious hospitality is evident throughout. It was originally built in 1926 as a residential building, so rooms are larger than average for NYC, and all have had face-liftings. All rooms come with fridge, two phones, cable TV, and rental movies. Swiss chocolates and toiletries complete the amenities. Complimentary limo service to Wall Street. Rates: from $200.

Once you've checked in at the **Elysee,** 60 East 54th St. 10022 (753–1066), you'll know why the hotel doesn't have to advertise, and why 90 percent of its bookings come from personal recommendation. The hotel is more like an inn. It's personally family-run, and each of the rooms in the 1927 brick building has its own name as well as number. Rooms are spacious, with comfortable brass beds, well-lighted desks, hair dryers, and a library of 350 video cassettes. Permanent residents have included Talullah Bankhead and Tennessee Williams. Right off the lobby is the noted Monkey Bar, with entertainment until 2 A.M. The Veranda restaurant serves northern Italian fare until 11 P.M. It's moderate to expensive and is an especially nice, quiet luncheon stop. Rate: $140—a real value.

Essex House, 160 Central Park South 10019 (484–5100). An old-world paneled lobby with spectacular floral arrangements invites lingering. With 700 rooms, the Essex House is one of the largest hotels along Central Park South's "hotel row." Separate desks for checking in and checking out help to avoid traffic jams. Rooms are spacious and come with a kimono-style robe and, for the weight conscious, scales. The Central Park South location is convenient for early-morning joggers, too. Devereux's restaurant, just off the lobby, specializes in continental cuisine. Rates: from $195.

Grand Hyatt, 42nd St. and Park Ave., 10017 (883–1234). Renovation of the old Commodore Hotel has resulted in a large (1,400 rooms), sleek, and dramatic setting. Design leans toward brass and glass modern. The Regency Club rooms hold special appeal for business visitors, with a private breakfast/cocktail hospitality lounge. Trumpets Restaurant (yes, replete with antique trumpets) serves American/continental fare. The Sungarden Restaurant, which juts out over 42nd Street, gives a feeling of dining in a plant-filled greenhouse. Try its bountiful Sunday brunch. The concierge can arrange for court time at an adjacent tennis club. Rates: $170.

The **Helmsley Palace,** 455 Madison Ave., at 50th St., 10022 (888–7000). This opulent, super deluxe establishment is the crown jewel of the five Helmsley-owned hotels in New York. It's large (962 rooms) and high (54 stories), towering above the 100-year-old Florentine Renaissance-period Villard Mansion, which cleverly has been made integral to the new construction. The public rooms are a wonder of rich paneling and marble inlay, all carefully restored. This is one of the prettiest places to stop for afternoon tea. Rates: $225–$275.

There are 640 rooms in the ideally located, modern **Helmsley Park Lane,** 36 Central Park South 10019 (371–4000). A high-rise building, the hotel is especially favored by visiting Europeans. Rooms are spacious and come with a mini-fridge. High tea in the Park Room has become so popular, especially during winter months, that we recommend reservations in advance. Rates: from $195.

Marriott Marquis, in the heart of the theater district at 1535 Broadway, between 45th and 46th streets, 10036 (398–1900). This offspring of the Marriott chain is modern and huge, with 1,876 guest rooms, 12 glass elevators, and a 37-story atrium. When construction commenced on the $400-million giant, much controversy developed because two landmark theaters had to be razed to accommodate the hotel. But in a gesture of good intent, Marriott incorporated a large modern theater within the hotel. And Schubert Alley, a thoroughfare in the midst of Broadway, was extended for another block right under the hotel. The hotel is topped off by a revolving, glassed-in restaurant, the only one in the city. Rates: from $220.

The superdeluxe **Mayfair Regent,** on Park Avenue at 65th St., 10021 (288–0800), is a jewel of a hotel radiating old-world charm. From the lobby's hand-painted ceiling panels to its cozy Orangerie tea room, the Mayfair Regent, better known abroad than here, makes you feel welcome. Where else does the staff not only remember your name but also remember guests' past preference for a feather or a foam pillow? Fit for a king? Absolutely! The M.F. happens to be a hotel favored by the King of Spain. There are only 165 rooms and many repeat guests, so reserve as far ahead as possible. Rates: from $210 for a room to $940 for the magnificent royal suite.

You might have trouble spotting **Morgans,** 237 Madison Ave., between 37th and 38th streets, 10016 (686–0300). The small, 154-room hotel purposely doesn't wear a sign in front and omits the word hotel from its name. That's to stress its air of informality and a sense of hominess. The creative genius of owners Steve Rubell and Ian Schrager (of Studio 54 and Palladium fame) is evident throughout this stylish inn.

Special touches include complimentary continental breakfast, thick terry robes, VCRs, and stereo cassette systems in each room. The friendly bar and oyster bar attract an eclectic crowd ranging from rock stars to financial types. Another nice perk—as a guest at Morgans, you're guaranteed entrance to the Palladium, not always an easy thing to pull off. Rates: $160–$195.

Opened in late 1984, the French-owned 470-room **Novotel**, 226 West 52nd St., 10019 (315–0100), reflects its Gallic roots. Modern rooms done in soft beigy pinks look out on Broadway or the Hudson. The lobby is on the seventh floor, built above an existing 1930s building. The Wine Bistro has an ongoing $6 wine-tasting happening, or you can taste from 20 wines available by the glass. In between sips, there are baguettes of bread and pâtés to nibble on. The Broadway Brasserie restaurant is open till midnight. Rates: $160.

Only one-half block from Carnegie Hall, **Parker Meridien,** 118 West 57th St. between Avenue of the Americas (Sixth Ave.) and Seventh Avenue, 10019 (245–5000), is French in feeling and image. (Air France is the owner.) Many of its 700 rooms have Central Park views and all are done in soothing gray or green contemporary tones.

Rooftop pool and jogging track and a full health club and squash courts are available to guests. Its elegant, neoclassic lobby and piano bar are an "in" cocktail hour meeting place for New York's "movers and shakers." Rates: $225–$260.

Westin Plaza, Fifth Ave. at 59th St. 10019 (759–3000). You can live in the Plaza if you wish. Just remember you're living in a restored, landmark hotel where, unfortunately, the personal-type service has given way to a more convention-type service. The rooms are of good size, nicely but not spectacularly decorated.

The Plaza is the Plaza, and a tradition; but if you're looking for up-to-date decor with the freshness of spring, perhaps you'd rather spend your hotel money elsewhere. But do go there for brunch or high tea in its Palm Court, or have drinks in the Oak Room, which is an institution. Rates: $200.

While not a clone of the Paris hotel of the same name, the superluxurious **Hotel Plaza Athenee,** 37 East 64th St., between Madison and Park avenues, 10021 (734 –9100), has the same ambience as the venerable Paris establishment. Opened in 1984 by Trust House Forte, with only 160 rooms, the beautiful hostelry deserves its name. The lobby has French antique furniture and hand-painted tapestry murals. Outside, a tailcoated *huissier,* or usher, leads guests in to sit down and register at an 18th-century desk. Obviously, the hotel is extremely popular with discerning travelers. There are room service pantries on every floor, and rooms have Directoire-style furniture and soft, soothing pastel decor. Rates: $275.

No conventioneers at the **Regency,** 540 Park Ave., at 61st St., 10021 (759–4100). The elite in the worlds of business and entertainment make the Regency their home away from home. From the foyer's Louis XVI-style decor and museum-quality tapestries to the marble and gilt room decor, elegance is the keynote. Each bath has a scale and phone, and the Regency Fitness Center has all the right equipment for the exercise-prone. You can even get a massage for $65 an hour. The 540 Park restaurant serves continental fare with a French flavor. Be sure to see the Seth Jacobs canvas, "Our Lady of Plenty," to the right of the restaurant's entrance. Rates: $195–$255.

Ideally located at 112 Central Park South 10019 (757–1900), **Ritz-Carlton** is a gem. It's just a short hop from some of the city's best shops. From the small and elegant lobby to the 240 spacious guest rooms—many with park views—all is sheer perfection. Rooms come with four-poster mahogany beds and the deft decorating touch of the incomparable Sister Parish. Impeccable, gracious service attracts repeat guests like Warren Beatty and Bette Davis. The Jockey Club restaurant (expensive) is wood paneled and warm, with a working fireplace and owner John B. Coleman's private collection of 18th-century oil paintings. Double-room rates from $225.

The small, comfortable **Sheraton-Russell,** 45 Park Ave., at 37th St., 10016 (685–7676), has an attentive staff and efficient concierge. The wainscotted lobby has a library and deep, comfy Chippendale furnishings. Be sure to visit the Judge's Chamber piano bar and lounge. Advance reservations are a must, especially for those rooms with a sweeping view of Park Avenue. Popular with business people checking the fashion market and related industries because of its proximity to the garment district. Parking available. Rates: $125–$220.

If it's hobnobbing with foreign diplomats you crave, consider **UN Plaza and Tower Hotel,** One United Nations Plaza, 44th St. and First Ave., 10017 (355–3400). Located across the street from the UN, this is a convenient place for diplomats to stay. Extra perks: free use of the 27th floor pool and health club. (Tennis court available for extra charge.) Free limo service to Wall Street, garment district, and Rockefeller Center. Advance reservations mandatory when General Assembly is in season, September and October. Rates: from $200.

Waldorf-Astoria, 301 Park Ave., between 49th and 50th streets, 10022 (355–3000), was recently restored to its 1930s art deco splendor. This large (1,800 rooms), luxurious hotel is a long-time favorite with presidents, kings, and, more recently, sheiks. Like fine wine, the Waldorf has improved with age. Rooms are spacious, individually decorated, and quiet. Peacock Alley is a popular jazz haunt and home to Cole Porter's very own piano. Overlooking the lobby, the Waldorf Cocktail Terrace serves tea from 2:30 P.M. to 6 P.M. and drinks until 2 A.M. Rates: $175. Tower suites: from $550.

Warwick, Sixth Ave. and 54th St. 10019 (247–2700). This old-world style property was built by William Randolph Hearst in the 1930s so that his paramour, Marion Davies, would be assured of a "room at an inn" near the old Ziegfeld Theater when she appeared there. Today, it's well run by a Hong Kong-based group who have kept its dignified tradition and simply, but nicely decorated, spacious bedrooms. Near theaters and museums and across the street from the huge New York Hilton. Rate: $150–$170.

Wyndham, 42 West 58th St. 10019 (753–3500), is a real find. This comfortable, small, privately owned and managed hotel does not advertise. For 20 years, customers have kept coming back . . . and back. Rooms are distinguished and cheery, with the accent on comfy country English decor. Loyal fans include Lena Horne, Hume Cronyn, and Mel Torme. No room service, but personal attentions of an exceptionally caring staff more than compensates. Basic American cuisine in Jonathon's Restaurant is inexpensive/moderate. Rates: only $105 double to $150 for a standard suite.

FINANCIAL DISTRICT

Vista International, 3 World Trade Center 10048 (938–9100). This large (825 rooms), modern-style hotel is in a great location for those doing Wall Street-related business. Three restaurants and bars draw fans, especial-

ly for ethnic food festivals on Fridays in the glass-enclosed Greenhouse. But the biggest plus is the physical
fitness center, pool, sauna, and jogging track atop the
hotel's 22nd floor. Work out in sight of the Statue of
Liberty. Rates: from $230, with special weekend "bar-
gains" available.

Restaurants

By Nancy B. Clarke

New York's restaurants are as diverse as its culture—representing every ethnic group at the United Nations and then some. With some 25,000 dining spots to choose from, you have endless gastronomic options to suit palate or purse. Most of the city's restaurants are located in the Midtown area. But outstanding dining is to be found almost anywhere, particularly in Soho, Tribeca, Greenwich Village, along Columbus Avenue, and the South Street Seaport. One of the city's most impressive restaurants, Windows on the World, sits atop the World Trade Center—a quarter of a mile high in the sky.

To be assured of a table, call ahead for reservations. For the new, "in" restaurants that do not take reservations, be prepared for a wait—a good opportunity to people-watch and socialize.

There's no excuse to go to bed hungry in the Big Apple. Restaurants, especially the new ones, are catering more and more to the late crowd. For example, the Odeon, in Tribeca, serves dinner until 12:30 A.M. and "supper" from 1 to 3 A.M.

For a memorable evening, and at a memorable price,

treat yourself to a dining experience at Lutèce, The Four Seasons, Café des Artistes, or Le Cirque.

The hot draw among the upward moving crowd is the large, bright, noisy, loft-like restaurants. Many are housed in former factories or warehouses, renovated to the latest style trend. Accent is on mass feeding and mass networking at places such as America, Ernie's, and Amsterdam's Bar & Rotisserie. If you plan to go to the theater after dinner, allow time for traffic delays in the congested theater district.

Many New York restaurants take a vacation break in the summer. Following an old European custom, some close during the entire month of August. Except for grabbing a bite at the corner pizza place, a pub, or a deli, always reserve a table in advance—whatever the time of year.

A New York tradition is Sunday brunch, accompanied by the *New York Times.* It's a leisurely, usually casual affair featuring anything from a featherweight cheese soufflé to a local favorite—lox, bagels, and cream cheese. Fit yourself into this local New York custom. The cost is reasonable, usually $7—$15 in neighborhood restaurants and pubs, slightly higher in hotels. Prices usually include Bloody Marys or mimosas and unlimited coffee.

Recent trends in cuisine lean heavily toward American regional, with special emphasis on Cajun, Tex-Mex, and the Southwestern style of grilling, smoking, and barbecuing. Coming to the forefront, too, is the plain and simple American cuisine that Grandma prepared so well. Pizzas are fast becoming "nontraditional." Expect to find them topped with anything from pesto sauce to goat cheese.

You can't possibly get to all of the eateries in the Big Apple. That's why our list is quite selective. Enjoy the awesome variety—and the glorious creations—of New York City dining.

We've classified restaurant costs based on a medium-priced appetizer, main course, dessert, and coffee. Cost per person also includes a moderately priced bottle of wine. *Superexpensive* is $65 per person and up; *Expensive,* $45–$65; *Moderate,* $25–$35; *Inexpensive,* $10–$20. Our costs *do not include* cocktails or cordials. A 15–20 percent gratuity is usual and there is an 8¼ percent tax on all food. A quick way to figure the tip is to double the sales tax.

When major credit cards are not accepted, we'll so note. For example, "No M," means the MasterCard is not accepted. Other abbreviations are: A, American Express; D, Diners Club; and V, Visa.

MIDTOWN

Okay, you don't feel like wandering too far astray from your Midtown hotel, but you still want to dine in style. Why not go for the best? Considered by many as *la crème de la crème* of Manhattan's restaurants is **Lutèce,** 249 East 50th St. (752–2225). This Alsatian restaurant is superb and absolutely not to be missed—if your budget can bear it. The menu is always fresh and imaginative, the service only rarely dips below gracious, and the setting, both downstairs and upstairs in the Petite Salon, is warm and intimate. Reservations are a positive must—sometimes taking months—so it would be wise to make them while planning your trip. It's a bit easier getting in for lunch, and easier on the pocketbook as well. Closed Saturdays in the summer, and Sundays all year. *Superexpensive.*

Just two short blocks north and two long blocks west is **The Four Seasons,** 99 East 52nd St. (754–9494). Not only is this continental restaurant a haunt of the rich and powerful, a place to see and be seen, but the food is excellent, as is the wine list. A seat by the reflecting pool in the formal dining room was once the "only" place to be; now, the somewhat less expensive Grill Room, opposite a shimmering stalactite bar, is considered to have equal panache. *Expensive* to *Superexpensive.*

A bit farther west, at 21 West 52nd St., is the renowned and recently refurbished **"21" Club** (582–7200), where you *cannot* reserve a table downstairs; they're held for, and consistently occupied by, those of Rockefeller-type stature. But the rest of this linked-together, hand-somely furnished town house is fair game. Note that despite the concerns of regular patrons over a refurbishing and a new menu, "21" still earns the praise of most critics and diners. Note, too, that lunchtime hamburgers are available at $21. But a stop at "21"—for a hamburger or caviar—is still considered one of life's little treats. *Super-expensive.*

Still a bit farther west, along New York's Rue de la Paix, you'll find the **Russian Tea Room,** 150 West 57th St. (265–0947). A tea room it's not; but Christmas every day it is, with decorations adorning the room all year round. The 60-year-old "RTR" serves the finest Russian cuisine in New York in a rich, pre-Revolution setting, complete with an antique samovar collection. Favorite dishes are blini served with sour cream and caviar, a succulent chicken Kiev and karsky shashlik. Especially popular for its after-theater supper, Sunday brunch, and *always* a favorite with art, film, and music patrons. (Carnegie Hall is a few steps east.) Jackets required for men. *Expensive.*

Just as expansive—and expensive—is **Petrossian,** one block north at 182 West 58th St. (245–2214), nestled in the magnificent art deco Alwyn Court building. Luxuriously furnished with gray kid leather banquettes trimmed with mink, and offering the Petrossian brothers' famed selection of caviar, this is a place to begin or end a splendidly romantic evening. Not so recommended is dinner, which easily tops $100 per person and can be disappointing. *Expensive* to *Superexpensive.*

In the mood for a thick, juicy steak? There are at least three steak houses in the Midtown area that rate our selection. **Palm Restaurant,** 837 Second Ave., near 45th

St. (687–2953), and its sister restaurant across the avenue, **Palm Too** (697–5198), serve up truly huge—and excellent—steaks and lobsters, as well as great cottage-fried potatoes and crisp onion rings. The Palm's no-reservation policy may mean long waits for tables. While waiting, check out the caricature-laden walls. Closed Sundays. *Superexpensive.*

There's a long-standing rivalry between **Christ Cella,** 160 East 46th St. (697–2479), and the Palm for the title of best steak in town. We won't take sides—they're both superb. So, too, is the roast beef served here and, like the steak, its dimensions are heroic. There are other choices on the menu, but the main event is definitely beef. Closed Sundays. *Expensive* to *Superexpensive.*

Another quintessential New York steak house is **Smith & Wollensky,** Third Ave. and 49th St. (753–1500). Noisy, always busy, macho atmosphere. But the steaks and chops are uniformly done to perfection, and loyal customers—many sports and advertising types—make S&W home. Upstairs room especially attractive with skylight and great floral arrangements. The Grill, on 49th Street entrance, serves lighter, more reasonably priced fare from 11:30 A.M. to 2 P.M. It's always lively. *Expensive.*

In the Rockefeller Center area, an old favorite is **Hurley's Saloon,** 1240 Sixth Ave. (765–8981). The owner of this establishment refused to sell his four-story building to the Rockefeller Center complex in the 1920s, so the saloon is surrounded by the center's skyscrapers. Excellent steaks, chops, and veal dishes served continuously from noon till midnight. Nice after-theater stop-off, and a favorite watering hole for NBC crews and staff. *Moderate.*

For a bit of old New York—and a bit of economizing as well—taxi, don't walk, over to the far West Side to **Landmark Tavern,** 626 Eleventh Ave. at 46th St. (757–8595). In a wonderfully restored 1800s saloon complete with pot-bellied stove, order shepherd's pie, soda bread, and hearty soups. Descendant of original owner Patrick Henry Carly wasn't daunted by Prohibition. He simply moved the bar upstairs to the family's living quarters and continued to quench customers' thirst. Now the upstairs speakeasy is a cozy dining room with period antiques and working fireplaces. Theater people, theater goers, and the crew from the QE2 make the Landmark a regular stop. Dinner service till midnight. A only. *Inexpensive* to *Moderate.*

Chances are you may have to wait in line to get into the **Hard Rock Café,** 221 West 57th St. (489–6565); but trust us, it's worth it. Billed as the only rock 'n' roll museum in the world, it is a one-of-a-kinder. An extra friendly place, Hard Rock features sophisticated "diner" food, like the famous barbecued pig sandwich or scrumptious "pie-in-the-sky" specialties. Diners are encouraged to wander about and inspect the memorabilia. Artifacts include Elvis's original Las Vegas jumpsuit and the purple coat worn by Prince in *Purple Rain.* A great after-theater stop. No reservations accepted. *Inexpensive.*

Big and bustling is **Café Un Deux Trois,** 123 West 44th St. (354–4148). A Parisian bistro in NYC? *Mais oui!* The noise level is always as high as the ceiling here because there is an energy, a sense that something exciting's going on all the time—because it is. No-frills French cooking is the rule of the day: poached and sautéed fish, steak pommes frites, stoutly seasoned birds. Your table comes equipped with crayons and a paper cloth so you can express your delight at having found such a fine eatery. Be sure to top off your meal with *profiteroles,* puff pastries with ice cream and sable-smooth chocolate sauce ladeled over all. *Moderate.*

Mike's American Bar and Grill is not that easy to spot at 650 Tenth Ave. (246–4115), with merely a gray sign over the front window. But plenty of people have found it out anyway. Inside, the decor changes according to seasonal whimsy, and the taped music is played very loud. The cuisine is Southern, with a special nod to South-of-the-Border specialties. Have a plate of Mike's special nachos to start, then select from whatever they've got on special—from fish to chicken to steaks. A welcome retreat to casual funk in this over-traveled, over-priced neighborhood. *Inexpensive.*

Great seafood restaurants in New York are curiously scarce. While at Rockefeller Center, 19 West 49th St., try the **Sea Grill** (246–9201). Soft colors, rich woods with accents of brass, and a view of the center's skating rink (outdoor cafe and garden in summer) and the gilded statue of Prometheus are the main attractions here. Unevenly successful is the menu, featuring red snapper, lobster, swordfish, and whole gingered fish. *Expensive.*

Beneath the main waiting room in Grand Central Station, off 42nd St. and Vanderbilt Ave., you'll find the vaulted ceiled **Oyster Bar** (490–6653). The clatter of cutlery and chatter of a roomful of diners bounces off the tiled floors and high tiled ceilings, and service borders on the rude. Nevertheless, the huge main room is one-of-a-kind grand, and the clams, oysters, and crabs year-round are all top notch. Quieter dining can be enjoyed in the adjacent *Saloon,* and quicker service at the sit-down counters. Closed Saturdays and Sundays. *Moderate* to *Expensive.*

At the southern edge of Midtown is one of the city's best seafood restaurants—**The Dolphin,** 227 Lexington Ave. at 34th St. (689–3010). Nestled in the quiet Murray Hill neighborhood, The Dolphin draws diners from far afield. Plump cherrystone clams or hearty chowder is followed by impeccably fresh fish, presented on a platter for inspection before being perfectly broiled or poached. Also available are lobsters and special seasonal fare. One caution: fish portions tend to be a bit small. Closed for lunch weekends. *Moderate to Expensive.*

Seafood combines with Creole cuisine at **The Barking Fish,** 705 Eighth Ave., between 44th and 45th Sts. (757–0186). Formerly Downey's, only the long, worn mahogany bar remains of this old newsmen's hangout that has been transformed into a New Orleans bistro, complete with ceiling fans, white latticework partitions,

and exposed brick walls. Chef Arthur De Cuir, of Baton
Rouge, keeps a watchful eye on such entrees as blackened red fish, seafood gumbo, and Creole jambalaya. A
Cajun brunch, on Sundays, features a three-piece Dixie-
land band. *Inexpensive.*

If it's Oriental food you crave, try **Chez Vong,** 220
East 46th St. (867–1111). Not one of your ordinary Chinese restaurants—which abound in New York—this
transplant from Paris boasts lace tablecloths, silk cush-
ions, bronze statues, a magnificent tiled mural, lacquered
chopsticks, and hand-painted plates. Though the kitchen
is a bit uneven, the Cantonese duck, Buddha's Delight
(stir-fried vegetables), chilled chicken with sesame sauce,
and sauteed abalone with sea cucumbers are generally
top drawer. (Price of abalone, in particular, is a bit steep.)
Expensive.

Japanese restaurants are flourishing all over Manhattan. A number are holes-in-the-wall, many are simply
decorated with Japanese touches, most include a sushi
bar, and a few are lavish affairs done in themes ranging
from Oriental splendor to art deco flash. Since it's difficult to go wrong, most New Yorkers tend to drop into the
one nearest at hand. In this area of town, our selection
is **Shinbasi,** 280 East 48th St. (661–3915). Though not
a drop-in place—reservations needed, especially at lunch
—Shinbasi is perennially popular. Sushi, tempuras, beef
and chicken teriyakis, tankatsu (breaded deep-fried
pork), and other selections can be had in the main dining
room, a tatami room, or the bar area (for parties of two).
Moderate.

At the two **Hatsuhanas,** 17 East 48th St. (355–3345)
and 237 Park Ave. (661–3400), the sushi is generally
agreed to be among the best available in New York. If
you care to see the masters at work, pull up a chair at the
bar and watch with what deftness the chefs maneuver
their knives. Although the prices are somewhat lower
(though still high for raw fish and seaweed) at lunchtime,

the place is packed—often a 45-minute wait. If you arrive right at noon, you might avoid the lunch crunch; or go at dinner when the pace is slower. *Moderate* to *Expensive.*

For good Italian fare, start off at **Il Nido**, 251 East 53rd St. (753–8450), with a combination of perfectly sublime pastas—angel hair, tortellini, and green noodles. This fashionable, northern Italian restaurant has some of the best food in town. Sure, the tables are a little too close and the noise level gets uncomfortable at times, but once you've tasted the dietary delights you won't mind. Save room for a lightly whipped zabaglione. Dinner served until 10:15 P.M. *Expensive.*

Guido Schiattarello has been presiding with pride over **Mama Mia**, 629 Ninth Ave. (974–9347), for 17 years. He's got checked cloths on the seven tiny tables and an artistic tribute to his homeport, Napoli, on the south wall. Lunch is a steal, with most entrees around $5. Dinner is likewise reasonable, with most entrees under $10. They make a wonderful sautéed calimari (ask if you don't see it on the menu) as well as a variety of veal dishes. *Inexpensive* to *Moderate.*

Sandro's, 420 East 59th St. (355–5150), features classic Roman cooking at its best in simple, palm-dotted surroundings. Try the zampone as a starter, then pick from the tripe, milk-fed lamb in the spring, exotic pastas, miniature gnocchi, and salads with scented vinegar and flavored oils. Dinners only. *Moderate.*

INDIAN CUISINE

For fine Indian cuisine, try **Akbar India**, 475 Park Ave., at 58th St. (838–1717). Northern Indian style, with the "hotness" level toned down to suit the palate. For an Indian "smorgasbord," order a mixed plate and try some new taste treats. Tandoor (clay oven) entrees are especially well prepared here. Dinner only on Sundays. *Moderate.*

At **Shezan,** 8 West 58th St. (371–1414), you'll descend a flight of stairs to a beautiful, mirrored room with soft gray carpeted walls. Favorite dishes are the hot Pakistani-Indian specialties. If you're uninitiated to Indian cuisine, attentive waiters will counsel you. Dinner only on Saturdays; closed Sundays. *Moderate.*

Also attractive, moderately priced, and of equally good quality, are **Bombay Palace,** 30 West 52nd St. (541–7777); **Raga,** 57 West 48th St. (757–3450); and **Tandoor India,** 40 East 49th St. (752–3334).

TEX-MEX

A taste of the trendy Tex-Mex cuisine, or vice versa, can be had at **El Rio Grande,** 160 East 38th St., at Third Ave. (867–0922). The Tex side is separated from the slightly more formal (in decor only) Mex side by a blue tile "river" running through the kitchen—the Rio Grande, of course. The place is usually mobbed five-deep at the bar, and though management keeps crowding in more tables, there's still a long wait to be seated, even with a reservation. The food, designed for those who are ambivalent about true Mexican food, is good; the margaritas are huge and lethal. *Moderate.*

More authentic Mexican is **Rosa Mexicano,** 1063 First Ave., at 58th St. (753–7407). Even before the first rave reviews came out, the mâitre d' here was turning away those without reservations and asking those with reservations to wait up to 20 minutes. But the wait was, and is, worth it. By all means, begin with the guacamole, then try one of the specials. The stucco-walled, slate-floored interior is accented with lavish displays, and though crowded in the bar area, it is relatively serene in the rear banquettes. *Moderate.*

UPPER EAST SIDE

Let's start our gastronomical tour of the East Side restaurants at the place that gave the area all its pizzazz nearly 20 years ago. **Maxwell's Plum,** 1181 First Ave., near 64th St. (628–2100), predates the recent trend toward large, boisterous, quirkily decorated restaurants. It's still very popular, and its food is still very good, with a menu ranging from hamburgers to rack of lamb. It's a long-time favorite for Saturday or Sunday brunch, too. Chic young New Yorkers also like Maxwell's decor of big ceramic animals, profusion of plants, mirrors and rococo flash. *Expensive.*

On the formal side—black tie on Friday evenings—is **Maxim's,** 680 Madison Ave., near 61st St. (751–5111). Pierre Cardin's art nouveau extravaganza, located in the Carlton House, has a turn-of-the-century, deliciously jaded Parisian look. Elegantly turned-out diners adorn the 200-seat Le Grand Salon, while gracing the French menu are such legendary Maxim dishes as quail eggs with caviar, mussel bisque, and salmis de canard. *Superexpensive.*

Four blocks to the north, at 58 East 65th St., is **Le Cirque,** a plush, haute cuisine French restaurant with a circusy mural of animals painted as human. Excellent service matches the meals, both of which attract the beautiful people. The regulars order a traditional yet offbeat specialty (traditionally not listed on the menu) of spaghetti primavera—one of the city's better versions of this trendy dish. Located in the Mayfair Hotel, this restaurant is closed Sundays. *Superexpensive.*

Celebrity spotting? Try **Elaine's,** 1703 Second Ave., at 88th St. (534–8114). That may be the only reason for visiting this restaurant, for the northern Italian fare is, at best, mediocre. Regulars—including writers, publishers, actors, and sports figures—populate the choice dining area, but those whom Elaine doesn't recognize occupy a side dining room. Elaine is fiercely protective of the privacy of her celebrated clientele. *Expensive.*

Rascals, 1286 First Ave., at 69th St. (734–2862), is a casual, friendly pub, specializing in simple American fare. A long, crescent-shaped oak bar, sawdust floors, and natural brick walls attract young doctors and nurses from nearby New York Hospital, as well as Mets baseball players. Busy bar trade subsides at dinner hour, picks up again after 10 P.M. Sunday brunch is an exceptionally good buy at $9.95 with unlimited mimosas or Bloody Marys. *Inexpensive.*

For Italian fare, everyone from the limo crowd to locals always seems to enjoy **Il Vagabondo,** 351 East 62nd St. (832–9221). Maybe it's due to good-natured cheers coming from the bocci court (the only one on the East Side), or to the waiters who seem to have as much fun as the patrons, or maybe it's just the careening pace of the place. At any rate, be prepared to wait at the bar for a table, do order the house wine with dinner, and by all means do come hungry. While the food doesn't pretend to be haute, it's honest and generously dispensed. *Moderate.*

The attractive dining room at **Fiorella Ristorante,** 1081 Third Ave., at 64th St. (838–7570), serves up a range of good pastas. The restaurant's greenhouse-style cafe area is a favorite for interesting individual pizzas, including a terrific pie with goat cheese and tomato-basil sauce. *Inexpensive* to *Moderate.*

Not fussy or fancy, **Mocca,** 1588 Second Ave., at 82nd St. (734–6470), offers friendly service and good honest heaping platters of Hungarian goulash, flanken, liver, stuffed cabbage, or the poetically named gypsy roast (pork). *Inexpensive.* For those who wish a quieter, candlelit setting, there's **Mocca Royale,** two doors away and one step up on the price scale. (737–2322). No credit cards. *Expensive.*

Pig Heaven is certainly only centimeters away from nirvana for those of porcine appetites. Decorated with dancing porkers of all degree and disposition, Pig Heaven, 1540 Second Ave. (744–4333), has been a favorite with the locals. The food is Chinese and extremely tasty. While prices are a bit high for Chinese, the preparation is so good, the portions are so substantial, and the place is so much fun that you'll be happy to pry open your wallet, so sit back and pork out. *Moderate* to *Expensive*.

Pamir, 1437 Second Ave. (734–3791) features Afghani food and faultless service in a neighborhood nearly spoiled by sameness. The small dining room is full of atmosphere and the scent of spices as you are seated, the sound is muted by Mid-Eastern wall tapestries. Afghani food incorporates a combination of spices—cardamon, coriander, ginger—creating an exotic variety of flavors; spicy, but not infernally hot. Lamb is featured, of course, but there is also an array of chicken and seafood specialties from which to choose. Start with a few different appetizers to pass around the table, and accompany your meal with a selection of their unusual fresh-baked breads. Coffee is thick, black, and very strong. *Moderate*.

UPPER WEST SIDE

As the only restaurant in Central Park, **Tavern on the Green,** at West 67th St. (873–4111), has perhaps the most exquisite setting in New York. Any time of year, the woodland view charms, as does the elegant and romantic decor, accented by Tiffany chandeliers, etched mirrors, tall silver candelabras, and banks of fresh flowers. From April through October, dining and cocktails can be had in an outside garden. Indoor offerings include the airy Pavilion Room with hand-painted murals of a French garden estate and twinkling cloud motif, and the Elm Room, with its famous glass-enclosed elm tree, mosaics, and chestnut paneling. Chefs tend to come and go; food reaches highs and lows, but leans toward the so-so. Nevertheless, the Saturday and Sunday brunch (10 A.M.–4 P.M.) is ever popular; dinner extends to 1 A.M. to accommodate theatergoers; and for many, the special sparkle of the surroundings seems to offset considerations of price against food value. *Expensive* to *Superexpensive.*

The flirty, semiclad nymphs in the seductive Howard Chandler Christy murals all seem happy in their surroundings at **Café des Artistes,** 1 West 67th St. (877–3500). And well they should be. This is one of the most beautiful dining places in New York City. Opened in 1915, the restaurant has been a lively gathering place for artists and writers ever since. Though now a more eclectic crowd meets there, the phantoms of Alexander Woollcott, Rudolph Valentino, and Noel Coward must lurk about. Despite the mirrored, elegant surroundings and impeccable table appointments, the cafe exudes the warmth and hominess of a European neighborhood bistro. The menu is French regional, with dishes such as pot-au-feu, rack of lamb with basil crust, or medallion of swordfish with bay scallops. *Expensive.*

The young owners of **Amsterdam's Bar & Rotisserie,** 428 Amsterdam Ave. (874–1377), were dubbed "pioneers" when they first opened their 1,800-square-foot restaurant on what was a nontrendy avenue a few years ago. The avenue now boasts standard poodles and flashy boutiques, and the restaurant is serving over 2,000 diners a week, with a special emphasis on chicken, plucked hot off the hissing wall-mounted rotisserie. *Inexpensive.*

For food with a Hispanic flair, **Victor's Cafe,** 240 Columbus Ave., at 71st St. (595–8599), is said to have the best Cuban cuisine in the city. Black bean soup, roast suckling pig, fried beef with garlic and onion, and paella are just a few of the entrees served in this lively non-stop cafe with jammed-in tables and good-natured, if harried, waiters. A favorite offshoot in the theater district is **Victor's Cafe 52,** 236 West 52nd St. (586–7714). Both *Moderate.*

MIDTOWN SOUTH AND THE VILLAGE

New York's only "floating restaurant," **The Water Club,** 500 East 30th St. (683–3333), is built atop two barges right on the East River. Despite its name, this isn't a private club, but a restaurant highly esteemed by New York's advertising and upscale business crowd. The lower deck has a fireplace and intimate dining scene; the upper deck (cash bar only) is more informal and has more reasonably priced food. Knockout sunsets make socializing on both decks a popular pastime. Dinner served until 11:15 P.M. daily, 10 P.M. on Sundays. *Expensive.*

Chiaki, 396 Third Ave. (696–4920), is an interesting interplay of culture and cuisine. The food is Japanese— out-of-the ordinary combinations of sushi and sashimi, plus a menu of other catchy, original dishes. The decor is decidedly Nippon Mod: high-gloss ebony black with wild paintings and sculpture highlighted by pin spotlights shooting out of the dark. The cool of the place is finally completed by a collection of new-wave and new-age soundtracks. This Japan is a far cry from deferential geishas shuffling around in sandals and kimonos. It's tough, slick, and ultra sharp. Moderate.

Set in Greenwich Village in an elegant carriage house once owned by Aaron Burr, is **One If By Land, Two If By Sea,** 17 Barrow St. (228–0822). Pre- and after-dinner drinks here can be sipped by the charming downstairs fireplace opposite the bar. Dining is on two floors, with the best view at a table near the upstairs balcony railing. Continental fare includes steak, veal, rack of lamb; wines are pricey. *Expensive.*

If you're looking for an island paradise on this most earthly of islands, set your course for **Caribe,** 117 Perry St. (255–9191). No matter where you're standing or sitting, there will be a wayward palm frond stuck in your ear and a frothy concoction stuck in your hand. Caribe is loaded with greenery and patronized by plenty of people who come from the Caribbean Islands and beyond. Try a Red Stripe beer with your meal of plantains, conch salad, and entrees with such picturesque names as jerked chicken (your waiter will explain). Of course, they play island music, so you can close your eyes and pretend you're beside an azure lagoon somewhere. No credit cards. *Inexpensive.*

Café de la Gare, 143 Perry St. (242–3553), is an exquisite bagatelle in a West Village setting. Barely half a storefront, the dining room is painted and lit to a soothing glow and hung with nice little pictures, and flowers adorn crisp tablecloths. The chef will send you an array of dishes inspired by classic French techniques, less formal, but no less successful. There is wonderful salmon, prepared according to the chef's seasonal whim, veal, and inspired presentations of game. There are a limited number of tables, so reservations are a must. No credit cards. *Moderate.*

French provincial food is featured at **Café Loup,** 18 East 13th St., in the Village (255–4746). Informal, with only 20 tables, this friendly eatery provides good French country food. Especially popular with neighborhood residents. Entrees, such as butterflied whole baby salmon, come with carefully prepared vegetables, and in generous portions. A small garden allows summer dining alfresco, with a background of classical music. Sunday brunch is hearty and reasonable. *Inexpensive* to *Moderate.*

A bit farther north and east is **Canastel's,** 229 Park Ave. South, at 19th St. (677–9622), an informal Italian-style restaurant. Though the fashion folk tend to be a fickle lot, at last notice they were adorning Canastel's en masse. Pretty women, handsome men at practically every table. And they all seem to know one another. Dress here is faded-jeans casual, the food is pasta and individual pizzas—both good—and the service is adequate. *Inexpensive* to *Moderate.*

Provence, 38 Macdougal St. (475–7500), has garnered a string of devotees in the short time it has been open just off Avenue of the Americas. Behind the bay of high windows is a most inviting dining room, soft-lit, and paneled with fine-carved mellow brown wood. Your meal is served by a crew of the sharpest, best-informed, most charming waiters in the city. Ask yours to suggest one of their selection of wines from the south of France. The menu is based on Provence's passion for the freshest ingredients, flavored with a judicious measure of seasonings and sauces. Ask about the daily specials—although the menu items are equally enticing. For dessert, perhaps a fruit tart with satiny cream, or a fruit ice livened by a dash of liqueur. There is garden seating in the back during nice-weather months. *Moderate.*

SOHO

A finer, less formal French fare is to be found at **La Gamelle,** 59 Grand St. (431–6695). Crowded with a most eye-opening array of locals late into the night, the bar up front is alive with loud and earnest conversation (in at least two languages); upstairs at the tables in back, you'll have the opportunity to scan the menu scribbled on blackboards around the room. The simple French cooking won't leave you exhausted by heavy sauces, but rather prepared to sample a soupçon of dessert with your demitasse. *Moderate.*

Abyssinia Restaurant, 35 Grand St. (226–5959). Abyssinia is the ancient name for the lands of Ethiopia, and while an Ethiopian restaurant may seem a bit strange these days, the food is delicious. Best to come with a crowd if you can. You sit on low stools around a poly-chrome woven-straw table onto which is set a huge round bowl lined with a thin layer of spongy, chewy bread. You use this bread as a utensil, scooping up the spicy fare served on top of the bread. All the while Ethiopian music plays in the background, the walls are hung with Ethiopian artwork, and your veins are coursed by a potent honey wine. You'll be transported.

Le Ferrandi, 462 Broadway (219–3300), is run by the French Culinary Institute, which is based in Paris. Its restaurant at the corner of Broadway and Grand Street is no finishing course for bored housewives, however, but a serious program preparing graduates to work at the finest restaurants in the country. The dining room is spacious and soft-lit by high windows. Soft jazz purls down from the ceiling and the walls are hung with a constantly changing array of works by local artists. The food is classic French and the menu changes frequently to give students experience in preparing a wide variety of dishes. Within this framework the students are gradually encouraged to extend basic techniques into new and untried territory, often with striking results. The price for a five-course dinner is $25; a five-course lunch is equally reasonable, as is a three-course meal. When the menu and the artwork change, Le Ferrandi hosts an evening of "Art and Cuisine." The artist and chef (often an invited guest) create an evening's menu to complement the artworks, with the proceeds going to a local charity. Call for information on upcoming "Art and Cuisine" events.

At **Amazonas,** 492 Broome St. (966–3371), a white piano, dramatically spotlighted, comes to life, along with accompanying instruments, after dinner. The menu is classic Brazilian, with grilled pork and steaks, Portuguese fish stew, shrimp dishes, and rice and beans. *Moderate.*

TRIBECA

In the Tribeca area, **Montrachet,** 239 West Broadway (219–2777), presents a simple backdrop of pale green walls and pinkish banquettes, where attractive diners are beautifully presented with reasonably priced light French fare. Among the specialties are red snapper, bass barigoule, roast duck, sweetbreads, eggplant, and thick crusty bread. At last visit, a special prix fixe dinner was hovering at only $19. *Moderate.*

Avid sports fans will find their fill at the **Sporting Club,** Hudson and Franklin streets (219–0900). An enormous video screen with a computerized scorecard dominates one wall of this cavernous former warehouse, while scattered strategically are a half-dozen TV monitors. The event of the day—football, boxing, baseball, etc.—is scooped up by satellite dish. Dressed in cheerleader outfits, waitresses dispense burgers as well as baby-back ribs, pasta dishes, steak, and a fish of the day. *Inexpensive.*

EAST VILLAGE AND LOWER EAST SIDE

Laugh with your kosher-style (but not kosher) meal at **Sammy's Roumanian Restaurant,** 157 Chrystie St. (673–5526). All the waiters there think they're comedians, but the food is not to be taken lightly—delicious chicken soup, blintzes, *karnatzlach* (a very garlicky sausage), and potted steak. Go in good health and enjoy! *Moderate.*

Great for Sunday brunch—especially that New York favorite, cream cheese and lox on bagel—is **Ratner's Dairy Restaurant** at 138 Delancey St. (677–5588). *Inexpensive.*

Johns, at 302 East 12th St. (475–9531), is the perfect place to pitch some woo with the one you love or are hoping to love. It is *molto romantico,* tile floors, dripping candles, scenes of the Old Country painted around the wall. The food is also guaranteed to ingratiate you with your dining partner. Try the antipasto for two to start, then perhaps some of their crispy garlic-laden bread (it's very strong, so to insure romance, make certain you *both* have some), then select a plate of pasta or one of their daily specials of fish or veal. Linger over your espresso to hold hands—take your time, the waiters understand. No credit cards. *Moderate.*

The Cloisters, at 238 East 9th St. (777–9128), is a sanctuary from East Village hecticness. This is especially true in the summertime when the Cloister's fountain-freshened garden is open. The place is appropriately decorated with stained glass and statuary, and soothing strains of classical music linger around the rose bushes. The food is generally good and inexpensive, tending toward lighter fare, pasta, and salads, although dinner specials are available daily. Brunch is especially popular here, so expect a wait. *Inexpensive.*

LITTLE ITALY

What's a trip to Little Italy without an Italian-style dinner? If you prefer the elegant, there's **SPQR,** 133 Mulberry St. (925–3120), right in the heart of the area. Northern and southern Italian cuisine served for lunch or dinner, although the food is considered so-so. Night club upstairs features dancing and name entertainment. *Expensive.*

One of the most popular Little Italy haunts is **Grotto Azzurra,** 387 Broome St. (673–6044). Food here is considered superior, though some are put off by the prices, in view of the simplicity of the decor and sawdust on the floor. No credit cards. *Moderate.*

A place for partying in Little Italy is **Puglia's,** 189 Hester St. (226–8912). Seating is at long, camp-style tables; homemade wine is served by the bottle; and the fare is hearty southern Italian. Sing-along routines on week-ends. No credit cards. *Inexpensive.*

Two favorite fresh seafood places are **Umberto's Clam House,** 129 Mulberry St. (431–7545), and **Vincent's Clam Bar,** 119 Mott St. (226–8133). Both very informal and both *Inexpensive.* For pastry and cappuccino, stop in at **Ferrara's,** 195 Grand St. (226–6150). Open and bustling till midnight. *Inexpensive.*

CHINATOWN

Though half the fun of a visit to Chinatown is selecting a restaurant based on one's instincts or mood of the moment, the downstairs room at **Tai Hong Lau,** 70 Mott St. (219–1341), is recommended for the indecisive. Here the fare is of Hakka/Hong Kong inspiration—pan fried bean curd stuffed with sausage; excellent deep-fried squid with hot pepper slivers; intriguing and beautifully arranged varieties of stir-fried vegetables; baby clams, cashew nuts, and pork rolled in lettuce leaves. No credit cards. *Inexpensive.*

While in Chinatown, do try the dim sum (dumplings stuffed with variations of meat, seafood, or vegetables) at **HSF Restaurant,** 46 Bowery (374–1319). These delicious tidbits, which you choose from a succession of trolleys, can serve as appetizers to a dinner or as main course lunch. *Inexpensive.*

FINANCIAL DISTRICT

When you go downtown to dine, go all the way down —and all the way up—to **Windows on the World,** 1 World Trade Center (938–1111). Perched atop the city's tallest building, 107 floors up, this lavish and stunning restaurant offers a wraparound view of the city, particularly exciting at night. The decor includes a rock-lined, mirrored reception chamber; a multitiered main dining room; mirrors and glass encompassing various dining rooms, cocktail lounges, and private rooms; lavish touches of brass, wood plants, and fresh flowers; and waiters resplendent in white uniforms with gold epaulets. The continental food and service, alas, don't always live up to the view. Reservations a must. *Expensive* to *Superexpensive.* On the same floor, the **Hors d'Oeuverie** is an internationally minded cocktail lounge and grill that can be less expensive if you eat and drink lightly, while enjoying the sights and listening to the piano music.

In the South Street Seaport area, the third floor of the newly opened Pier 17 Pavilion is the dramatic setting for the highly popular **Liberty Cafe,** 89 South St. (406–1111). From tiered seating, everyone gets a sweeping view of the East River and a glimpse of the New York harbor. The pavilion, with its open views, juts out over the water, so you get the sensation of being on a river vessel. Fare is American regional, with seafood grilled over mesquite, a leading favorite. Dinner is served until midnight. *Moderate* to *Inexpensive.*

A favorite haunt for singles in the South Street Seaport is **Roeblings,** 11 Fulton St. (608–3980). Although noted for its hurly-burly and friendly bar scene, Roeblings' casual and unpretentious dining room must be doing something right. (Mayor Koch has been a regular luncheon patron.) Specialties of the house are blackened red fish, Norwegian salmon, and a fresher-than-fresh fillet of sole. Note though, Roeblings at times is not for quiet dining. The noise from the bar, particularly at happy hour, can make the place not conducive to networking or interacting. The outdoor cafe is popular in summer. *Moderate.*

SOMETHING SPECIAL,
SOMETHING ORDINARY . . .

New Yorkers tend to take for granted the abundance and variety of restaurants the city has to offer. For the visitor, here are a few fun places to eat, some of which fail to fit into any particular category. Most don't take credit cards and most are in the *Inexpensive* category.

The finest soul food in town can be found at **Sylvia's** in Harlem, 328 Lenox Ave. (534–9414). It's worth a cab trip uptown to try Sylvia's southern-fried chicken, barbecued spare ribs, stuffed pork chops, and homemade cornbread. Closer to Midtown, **Jezebel's,** 630 Ninth Ave. at 45th St. (582–1045) also boasts a fine Southern kitchen.

Tapas, those delectable Spanish appetizers, are the latest rage in New York, and the best of these can be enjoyed at a tapas bar at **El Internacional,** 219 West Broadway, Downtown (226–8131).

On the more exotic side, the **Tamu Indonesian Restaurant,** 340 West Broadway, Downtown (925–2751), serves a traditional Indonesian Rijstaffel buffet banquet. A new branch was recently opened in the Village at 248 West 14th St. (929–3564).

More in the New York style is the **Carnegie Delicatessen,** 854 Seventh Ave., at West 55th St. (757–2245), setting for Woody Allen's *Broadway Danny Rose.* Corned beef hash and mile-high deli sandwiches are tops here. Always crowded and always bustling. Nearby and just as good is **Stage,** 834 Seventh Ave. (245–7850), which attracts a large after-theater crowd—from both sides of the stage. Surly waiters are considered part of the fun.

Two breweries, of all places, are attracting the young, upwardly mobile and middle-aged alike for sandwiches, desserts, and beer on tap, as well as other beverages. The **Manhattan Brewing Company,** 40 Thompson St., Downtown (219–9250), also features a third-floor restaurant, with seafood a specialty. In Midtown, the

New Amsterdam Tap Room, 235 Eleventh Ave., at 26th St. (255–4100), similar fare is offered, with tours of the brewery slated to begin in 1986 at 1, 3, and 6 P.M.

THEATER DISTRICT

There are lots of good theater area restaurants, particularly along Restaurant Row on 46th Street. **Charlie's** and **Orso's,** 263 West 45th St. (354–2911) and 322 West 46th St. (489–7212), respectively, are two very popular and reasonably priced suggestions. Charlie's, a pub specializing in hamburgers and mobbed before and after the theater, not only caters to show-goers, but gets its share of theater stars as well. Orso's is a small, crisp bistro—far quieter than Charlie's—offering an inventive array of individual pizzas and pastas. Both *Inexpensive.*

Shopping

By Nancy B. Clarke

For the serious shopper and for the browser, shopping in New York is like no other place in the world.

Gucci, the finest in Italian leathers, shoe, belt, and handbag, stands proudly at Fifth Ave. and 54th St. Their high-priced, highly prized goods are on display in the store, entrance on Fifth Avenue.

Around the corner, at the 54th Street entrance, you can take the elevator to **Gucci on Seventh.** Here—on the seventh floor, of course—you'll find genuine Gucci articles at clearance-sale prices. This little-known outlet is ideal for gift buying.

Meanwhile, a few street corners away, as well as at other street corners throughout the city, are other "Gucci's," guarded by street vendors with one eye cast for a sale and the other for the fuzz. "Genuine copy—half the price of other Gucci!" proclaims one young entrepreneur.

New York, New York, it's not only one helluva town, but it offers everything—including the Brooklyn Bridge —for sale. Moreover, the type of merchandise you're seeking can often be determined by the neighborhood. Major department stores, for instance, are located in

Midtown. So are the fine shops along Fifth Avenue, as well as the diamond dealers along West 47th Street, just off Fifth Avenue. Upper East Side features smart boutiques and high-priced galleries, while the West Side, particularly along Columbus Avenue, adds more and more of the trendier shops. The Lower East Side, meanwhile, offers discount electronic and electric appliances, as well as clothing and textiles.

If it's books you're seeking, major chains are represented throughout the city, but it should prove worthwhile for a short trip below Midtown to **Barnes & Noble,** on both sides of Fifth Avenue, at 18th Street. The main store, on the east side of the avenue, is known for its vast array of scientific material and college textbooks. Across the avenue, the Sale Annex has a huge selection of many categories, including best-sellers, at well below list price. The best of the used-book stores is **Strand,** at Broadway and 12th St. Books here include, besides some rare books and the over one million used books, mint-condition reviewers' copies at half price.

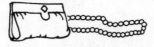

To take you on a shopping "tour" of the city, we conducted our own highly selective, highly unscientific poll, with some of the most savvy New Yorkers we know. We put the question to them: "You have only one day to shop in New York City, and then you can never—nay, never—spend your dollars, francs, kopeks, pesos, marks, here again. One day, we say. Where will you go to shop?"

Would you believe that on almost every list reigned **Bloomingdale's!** That famous emporium covers the square block between 59th and 60th streets and between Lexington and Third avenues.

New Yorkers must be romantics at heart, because the next highest rating was the windows at **Tiffany's,** Fifth Ave. and 57th St. Early, early in the A.M. when, like Holly Golightly, you're fighting off the mean reds, or during the rush of weekday crowds, the windows of Tiffany's are a work of art unto themselves. A handful of emeralds casually thrown in between rocks . . . diamonds used to outline a child's sand castle . . . hidden waves splashing over all.

If you're in town during the Christmas shopping season (after Thanksgiving), be sure to drop by their stocking-stuffer counter on the second floor. You'll be surprised at what you can find for $25 and under. Choose from a sterling silver Big Apple bookmark or a silver key ring—at $24 each. A set of playing cards, from an exclusive 1879 Tiffany design, is $10. There are up-to-date items, too. One favorite is the slim, diamond-textured ballpoint pen, for $21. And packaged in Tiffany's famous blue box, too. Just across the avenue is **Bergdorf Goodman,** always ready to accommodate with that chic and expensive gift or *pour-moi* purchase. A bit farther down the avenue, at 39th St., the Christmas-window decorations at **Lord & Taylor** are a special treat—so is its fine clothing by American designers.

Of course, another knowing New Yorker in our survey nodded and said, "Tiff's windows are wonderful. But I prefer **Cartier.** Inside Cartier, Fifth Ave. at 52nd St., those little gold pinky rings, chains, or tank wristwatches are ideal for something amusing."

The same mink-lined boots that took that shopper to Cartier, also take her to **Bolton's,** with 14 stores throughout the city. Nine are in Manhattan. Prices are well under those of the major department stores.

Some of the larger department stores still have their devotees. **Macy's** reigns supreme for household goods (although roller skates would be helpful to cover their huge emporium at Herald Square, 34th Street and Broadway). And when feet fail, there's a branch of *P.J. Clarke's* restaurant here as well. Not-so-trivial-pursuit: Did you know that Macy's is our oldest department store, founded in 1858?

Henri Bendel's, on West 57th St., just off Fifth, has no French pronunciation in its name. But it has French flair—and fit. Small bosoms, small waists, and no hips help. But the clothes are wonderful; the departments (like the designs) small and select. It's not for everyone, but then it never intended to be.

Trump Tower, nearby, at 56th St. and Fifth Ave., with a multilevel shopping arcade, has been a disappointment to most. The boutiques are international and superexpensive, but with all that pizzazz we were expecting . . . well . . . pizzazz! And so far, much ado about not much.

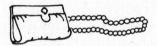

Columbus Avenue from the low 70s to the high 80s has taken off faster than a speeding bullet. Twenty years ago, this was the place you came to be mugged. Then Lincoln Center opened in the 1960s; restaurants followed for the pre- and apres-theater crowd, and sometime in the early 1980s, the new Columbus Avenue "happened." Now the feeling is European . . . the fashions are mainline Italian (with some French) . . . the upscale clientele is streetwise and clotheswise.

Botticelli, at 416 Columbus Ave., has everything from Italy, including a stunning dark French rabbit coat with chocolate leather sleeves for $2,300. Gloves, handbags, belts, collected bits of this and that. Some glitz; all quality.

Sandi Lynne, owner of **Courts and Sports,** at 410-16 Columbus Ave., was the first of the new wave to open on the avenue. Her goods are devoted to tennis, ski, and swim wear, and all are imported.

Beau Brummel, at 410 Columbus, is the 80s version of the name. Owner Sol Laxer knows his customer well, and he's very fashion-conscious. Almost everything is imported from Italy, with a few pieces from Germany. For about $1,000, Laxer can give any man one full version of the Beau Brummel look.

Laura Ashley at 398 Columbus Ave. brings back shades of the Victorian and Edwardian eras, even in this London-based company's step-stores in Paris, Geneva,

Milan, Zurich, Vienna, Amsterdam, and Bath. Time stopped at Laura Ashley, both in the very ladylike clothes and in the home design center.

Take a shopping break and restore your stamina with some of the exotic snacks offered by the sidewalk food vendors. Choices range from delicate quiches to hearty chowders.

La Merceria, at 328 Columbus Ave., has some French high-quality items mixed in with Italian high-quality items. Their specialty is Italian hand-knit sweaters that range from $100 to $300.

To Boot, at 256 Columbus, has the very finest in footwear for men. Beautifully cut men's shoes around $200.

Tianguis, at 284 Columbus, is folk art to be worn by those who appreciate. Many of the human and animal figures were inspired by pre-Columbian art, and have been translated onto fabric. Ericka Peterson's motifs include cats, birds, eyes, lips, arrows, snakes. Many of the hand-painted fabrics have been done by the Harlem Textile Works, but there are pieces like a tassel dress of corduroy and taffeta from England for $120, or a hand-knit cotton sweater for $95. But the pièce de résistance has to be the real Mexican frog, crinkled, preserved, with a zip added to make him a zip of a purse at $30!

When you move over to Madison Avenue and the really big time in the spending department, start with lunch at **Maxim's** (see *Restaurants* section). This branch of the Paris-renowned restaurant opened in 1985, and lunch for two (without wine) should run about $60 or $70. Now you're ready for the heavily French-accented boutiques on Madison Avenue.

St. Laurent For Men picks up the beat at 543 Madison (near 55th St.). Exquisitely tailored suits, all expensive, along with all the fashionable accessories.

Georg Jensen, 683 Madison, at 61st St., is Danish, "By appointment to the Royal Court." This silversmith is quite special, and its china, crystal, watches, and clocks, as well as the sterling for which it's known, make the finest of gifts for yourself or someone special.

Julie's, at 687 Madison, is very much in the vanguard, even for New York. Julie Schafler Dale has been selling "wearable art" for 12 years now, all crafted by U.S. artists. The pieces might be a simply spectacular silk skirt and top, hand-painted by an ancient Japanese method but of modern design—$900, and worth it! Or, it might be as 1980s as a Susanna Lewis coat, based on the computer. The coat is called Syntax Error, with panels reading Load, List, Run, Fly. As Mrs. Dale says, "These pieces are not done for the commercial market, but for the joy of creating."

The Limited, on the corner of 62nd and Madison Ave., opened its designer doors in the winter of 1985, housing many upscale American designers. There's an exclusive line by Kenzo, a boutique of designer lingerie, and other surprises over three heavily carpeted floors.

The French connection continues with **Lanvin,** at 701 Madison Ave. And it's interesting to know that even if you're planning a trip to Paris, you may want to buy here. The New York-sent designs have much more color than those in the City of Lights! Many of the styles are the same, but fabrics and color are brighter over here. As to price, well, here they won't tell the cost range. . . . Possibly the old Vanderbilt line applies: "If you have to ask the price, you can't afford it."

Charles Jourdan, at Madison and 66th, has the very best quality in ladies shoes of all designs. This year, a basic (more or less) leather high-heeled pump is around $150.

Next door, at 765 Madison, **Tennis Lady/Tennis Man,** has everything in clothing or equipment for the tennis- or squash-playing grown-up person. (No togs for tots.) This is the flagship store for the company that had over 30, at last count, scattered over the U.S. Names such as Fila, Ellesse, Tail, Head, Sergio Tacchini, tempt you to really improve your backhand.

While not on the hit list, the aptly named boutique, **Therapy,** at 799 Madison, is what some New York shopping is all about. Cheaper, actually, than New York psychiatrists.

Emanuel Ungaro, 803 Madison Ave., the stateside version of big-sister in Paris, is carrying exquisite hand-painted silk, slightly quilted long jackets for $1,975. A basic wool jersey chemise in magenta or black runs about $675.

Veneziano, 819 Madison Ave., brings the most incredible sweaters and knits from Italy. If you can buy just one this year, stop here before deciding.

Pierre Balmain offers its signed collection at 795 Madison Ave. . . . **Saint Laurent's Rive Gauche** had a corner to itself at 855 Madison Ave., which may explain why **Ralph Lauren** opened at Madison and 72nd!

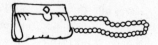

If it's bargains—and bargaining you're looking for—take a bus on Second Avenue downtown to the Lower East Side. There, nestles the tucked-away shops of Orchard Street. From Houston Street south, it's high-ticket apparel items with some of the zeros knocked off the price tags.

Since the ownership is Orthodox Jewish, closing hours are before sundown on Friday. Here, it's "never (open) on Saturday," but all shops are open on Sunday, as well as weekdays. Hours: 9 A.M. to 5 or 6 P.M. Most Orchard Street stock is crowded and cramped, and you really have to know your labels.

One of Alyse's favorites—our New York-born guide who shops the area constantly and consistently—is **Lace Up,** at 110 Orchard St. This savvy shoe and boot store has been in business over 20 years. The labels (with 25 to 30 percent off uptown prices) read: Charles Jourdan, Yves Saint Laurent, Bandolino, Evan-Picone, Anne Klein, Bruno Magli.

Forman's has three shops in the area, but Alyse beelines to the designer apparel at 92 Orchard St. Sections are marked: Evan-Picone, Pierre Cardin, Bill Blass, Calvin Klein.

We were hooked by Elliott Kivell, the owner of **D & A,** at-home items for men and women, at 22 Orchard St. —25 to 30 percent off is standard. And lingerie names for women are familiar: Lily of France, Olga, Maidenform, Danskin. Men's labels read Jockey, BVD, Christian Dior.

Insiders take note: Men's robes on women are comfy, and sexy!

Other favorites on Orchard Street that get the Alyse-tested stamp of approval are **Fishkin Knitwear,** for sportswear, at 63 Orchard St. This season, a Harvé Benard all-wool coat is in the $240 category. Other "known" names are Liz Claiborne, Jones New York, Saint Tropez West, Carole Little. All are well off department store prices.

Lolita, at 70 Delancy St., also displays lingerie labeled Christian Dior, Lily of France, Olga. **Shulies,** at 175 Orchard, has the very avant-garde Hatari designs. **Fine and Klein Handbags,** at 119 Orchard, has the best in designer purses at the very best prices. Another good bet is **Ber-Sel Handbags,** at 79 Orchard St. **A. Altman,** 182 Orchard, is chockablock with high-fashion fashions for women, but even designer hangers entangle in the minispace. Clothes and customers stand sideways here.

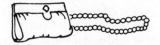

In the Soho, Noho, Tribeca area (still, way downtown . . . a map is very useful), another New Yorker, Claire, discovered **Victoria Falls,** at 451 West Broadway, where we lost our hearts (and credit cards) to an '80s version of the '20s look. A Lauren Bacall-slink long satin dress can be combined with a matching long satin jacket for $300. A beaded flapper number in silk crepe is yours for $400, or a genuine '20s antique lace wedding dress—the real thing—goes for $3,500.

Some of Bianca Jagger's designs hang at **Paracelso,** at 432 West Broadway. Others show a strong Indian and Southeast Asian influence. Interesting dresses run around $100; scarves are from $40 to $80.

The antique clothes craze continues—and it's strong everywhere—at **Back in Black,** 123 Prince St., where dated robes from Japan, with hand-embroidery ($75), would make a smashing at-home outfit over a simple sweater and slacks. There are also early Americana patchwork quilts, and a collection of costume jewelry. (You can skip the latter.)

The Gallery of Wearable Art, 480 West Broadway, offers one-of-a-kind clothing that is art—high-priced art. Owner Bonnie Storch Kupris feels that "after years of uniform dressing, American women are ready to make a statement." That statement could run as high as a $7,300 mink coat by Parisian George Coulount Jos that reverses to a hand-painted, kaleidoscopic pink and purple skin side. Or, check out sweaters by calligrapher Linda Mendelson that can run as high as $2,500. With these prices, they understand if you're "just looking."

Possibly the most interesting of New York's many and deservedly famed art galleries are in Soho, Noho, and Tribeca. But you should be aware that these are now well-established galleries, some of which are children of Midtown parent galleries. This is the big time in the art world, and you should look in where some of the best artists show.

Anton van Dalen, who lives in New York, but comes from Holland, is one of the best. His work often shows at the **Edward Thorp Gallery,** 103-105 Prince St., along with other contemporary American painters and sculptors. This is the gallery that sometimes has jazz at its frequent openings, and it's well worth your time. (Note: almost all Soho galleries have similar hours, Tuesday through Saturday, 10 A.M.–6 P.M.)

Two **Leo Castelli** galleries, at 420 West Broadway and 142 Greene St., are relatives of a major Uptown gallery. At both, you might see the works of artists who came into their own in the '60s—Robert Rauschenberg, Jasper Johns, Claes Oldenburg, Andy Warhol. From the early '70s, the galleries show large-scale paintings (some 10 feet tall), some by Keith Sonnier, Edward Ruscha, Bruce Nauman; or newer '80s artists such as David Salle.

Another highly respected gallery in the Soho area is the **Paula Cooper Gallery,** at 155 Wooster St. Just a scattering of its major artists are Jennifer Bartlett, Jonathan Borofsky, Elizabeth Murray, Joel Shapiro, Carl Andre, Lynda Benglis, Peter Campus, Robert Gober.

It's possible to attend openings of exhibits at galleries like **Ronald Feldman Fine Arts Inc.,** at 31 Mercer St., if you just happen to time it right. This gallery, as well as others, changes exhibits about every six weeks, and openings are held early Saturday evenings. About 25 contemporary American and European artists are represented in their ground-floor gallery.

In the "top ten" of the highly respected, highly priced Soho galleries, with major artists, are the **Nancy Hoffman Gallery,** at 429 West Broadway, the **Monique Knowlton Gallery,** at 153 Mercer St., and the two-floor expanse of the **Phyllis Kind Gallery,** at 136 Greene St.

Another knowing friend, Rebecca, married to an international artist, told us about the "artists' artists" who show in the now-being-discovered A, B, C, and D avenues of the East Village. "No outsiders come here," sighed Rebecca. "At least they didn't. But now look at the limo lineup for an opening of the Gracie Mansion Gallery! It's bigger than at Mayor Koch's official Gracie Mansion!"

When we checked with owner, Gracie Mansion (?!) of the **Gracie Mansion Gallery,** at 167 Avenue A, and the **Gracie Mansion Museum Store,** at 337 East 10th St., it turned out to be true. She was an artist, like many others, forced to move from the now high-rent Soho/ Noho/Tribeca area. She turned her apartment into a gallery, and did her show in an overly-large bathroom! Now, she shows artists in the $500 to $25,000 range at her Avenue A gallery, and artists $200 and under at the Museum Store. Just a scattering of her major talents are: Rodney Alan Greenblat, Stephen Lack, David Sandlin, David Wojnarowiz, Rhonda Zwillinger. Outsiders are also welcome to her gallery openings, if your timing is right—about every month, and always on a Thursday.

Another favorite among the artists themselves is the **Ex-Voto Gallery,** Avenue A at East 6th St. It has folk art from around the world: folk art from India; wrestling gear from Mexico; voodoo flags, bottles, and banners from Haiti.

While you're in the East Village neighborhood, check out two galleries that specialize in political and sociological works—**P.P.O.W.,** at 216 East 10th St., and **Civilian Warfare** at 155 Avenue B. Not political, but worth a stop is the **Piezo Electric Gallery,** at 437 East 6th

St. It shows young American artists who are just starting to make it in the $200 to $20,000 price range.

But if you don't have the big bucks to blow on a painting, drop in at the **Pop Shop,** 292 Lafayette St., just south of Houston. The Pop Shop is Keith Haring's own outlet for his graffiti-geometric babies, doggies, trees. Haring also sells items created by Kenny Scharf, Stefano, and other like-minded artists. Haring painted the place: top to bottom, stem to stern, and staffs it with hip-hoppers who play baaad music during business hours (12–7 P.M. Tuesday–Sunday). Grab up some signature T-shirts, refrigerator magnets, inflatable babies, jewelery, and many other items you cannot possibly live any longer without. Prices are pretty reasonable for works of art.

Before all is seen and shopped, you may be wondering, "What does one wear when shopping in the Big Apple?" The answer can be "almost anything that's right for the season, and that includes walking or running shoes." Or, it could be the Upper East Side "uniform" that still holds . . . designer jeans, designer boots, and a mink jacket for the ladies. That's life in the fast lane.

Nightlife

By Kathleen Beckett

They don't call New York "The City That Never Sleeps" for nothing. You'll see why as you set out to explore New York's nightlife: a potpourri of every possible pleasure known to man—and then some.

The wilder shores of night are nowhere better experienced than in the clubs: a crazy collection that runs the gamut from seedy little rooms lit by bare lightbulbs to extravaganzas that put Las Vegas's glitzy pleasure palaces to shame. Some observations apply to all these places: you should call first for a rundown of times, prices, etc.; the doors tend to open around 10 P.M., but the action doesn't really start up till midnight; the music is taped and accompanied by various video displays; just as many people mill around with a drink in hand as burn up the dance floor; most people are dressed in black, so if you're in doubt about what to wear, just slip into anything black (a T-shirt is as good as a designer dress or suit—maybe even better); you'll be made to feel like a fool outside trying to get in. A suggestion for breaking the barrier: be polite but firm, aggressive, and confident. Don't stand back—go straight to the bouncer and ask in a pleasant but no-nonsense voice to enter, please. Act as if it is your birthright to be let in. Good luck.

Entry fees vary from $5 for offbeat little clubs to $20 for the biggies. Drinks are steep—approaching $10 a toss. But the show at these places is usually splendid—all the creatures of the night are there for your wonderment.

The Tunnel (220 12th Ave., 714–9886) is actually eked out of a former warehouse that trains actually pulled in and out of—some of the tracks are still there. Yet another mega-dance palace, the Tunnel features a dance floor in a very long, narrow room. You can sit above or stand beside and sip and stare at the late-night-ers cutting capers to the typically less-than-inspired dj's offerings. This is not to downplay the Tunnel: It's a per-fect place to go exploring with little sitting rooms deco-rated like plush opium-den playgrounds, corridors leading to nowhere, and powder rooms stashed away where you'd least expect to find them. Not to be missed is the laser light show emanating from about 50 yards down those train tracks. Twin lasers are set up at about the height of the headlight of an oncoming locomotive, emitting a multicolored, multishaped, multimetamor-phosizing beam of light—you'll know just how Anna Karenina felt.

The mammoth **Palladium** (126 East 14th St.; 473–7171), brought to you by Steve Rubell and Ian Schrager, the duo who gave the world Studio 54, offers level after level of design and art: a huge lit-from-underneath stair-case, sleek banquettes, giant video screens, Jean-Michel Basquiat and Keith Haring murals, and pay phones deco-rated with day-glo paint and plastic dinosaurs by Kenny Scharf.

If you are into an even heavier concept—God—the **Limelight** (47 West 20th St.; 807–7850) is for you. The owners gutted the pews from a wonderful old 19th-cen-tury church where the Astors and the Vanderbilts used to pray, and constructed a jungle gym of ramps and staircases in their place, so you can dance in the belfry next to the stained glass windows and organ pipes.

Neighboring **Private Eyes** (12 West 21st St.; 206–7770) is small, sleek, and lined with what seem to be a zillion video sets showing cartoons, movies, and music videos. It's a dance hall with video wallpapering.

If transvestites stripteasing on top of the bar is your cup of tea, try the **Pyramid Club** (101 Avenue A; 420–1590), one of the East Village's more "established" boîtes with live acts. It's small, it's sweaty, and the bouncer stamps your hand at the entrance just like at a high-school dance—but high school was never like this.

CBGB & OMFUG (315 Bowery; 982–4052) is perhaps the most famous of the small, sweaty Downtown clubs; it's an institution where Blondie and the Talking Heads cut their teeth.

For live music, one of the liveliest places is **The Ritz** (119 East 11th St.; 254–2800). The former ballroom is filled with dancers before, during, and after shows (which tend to start around midnight, no matter what they say) featuring musicians that invariably become the big names in rock. Til Tuesday and The Hooters sang their hearts out in this smaller setting before going on to the big concert halls; Tina Turner practiced for her comeback here, and Sting tried out his solo act.

When it comes to the big concert halls, check **Madison Square Garden** (4 Pennsylvania Plaza; 564–4400) and **Radio City Music Hall** (Sixth Ave. and 50th St.; 757–3100). Another smaller theater with a good lineup is the **Beacon** (2130 Broadway; 787–1477). Smaller still is the legendary **Bottom Line** (15 West 4th St.; 228–7880), where you can eat burgers and drink beer as you watch the next Bruce Springsteen (who, by the way, got his start in these hallowed halls) work out. And, if you are a country-and-western fan, head to the **Lone Star Cafe** (61 Fifth Ave.; 242–1664)—it's the building with the iguana on the roof—for great blues and country music, and great chili to boot.

For a night of jazz, head to Greenwich Village and its small, often smoky little clubs serving up the big names in the industry: **Village Gate** (160 Bleecker St.; 475–5120); **Village Vanguard** (178 Seventh Ave. South; 255–4037); **Sweet Basil** (88 Seventh Ave. South; 242–1785); **Bitter End** (149 Bleecker St.; 673–7030); **Fat Tuesdays** (190 3rd Ave.; 533–7902); **Blue Note** (131 West 3rd St.; 475–8592); **Bradley's** (70 University Place; 228–6440); and **Lush Life** (corner of Bleecker and Thompson streets; 228–3788). In Midtown, try **Michael's Pub** (211 East 55th St.; 758–2272) especially if you are a Woody Allen fan—he often plays his clarinet there on Monday nights.

For laughs, head to a comedy club—more and more, a favorite form of entertainment in the city—and let the Steve Martin or Bill Cosby of tomorrow try to get you to crack a smile. Chances are that someone in a vast rundown of hopefuls will tickle your funnybone. **The Improvisation** (358 West 44th St.; 765–8268) is granddaddy of them all, sending Robert Klein, David Steinberg, and Richard Pryor on the road to fame and fortune. Other good places to try: **Caroline's** (332 Eighth Ave.; 924–3499); **Catch a Rising Star** (1487 First Ave.; 794–1906); **Comic Strip** (1568 Second Ave.; 861–9386); **Dangerfield's** (1118 First Ave.; 593–1650)—Rodney's place where he does periodic stints, and **Comedy U** (86 University Place; 206–1296).

For even more laughs, try bowling—New York style. If you packed your '50s prom dress or leopard dinner jacket, slip it out and on and head to **Bowlmor Lanes** (110 University Place; 255–8188), where the Stray Cats filmed one of their music videos, for a night of bowling until 1 A.M. weekdays; 4 A.M.—with music—on Fridays and Saturdays.

Just want to sit back with a drink? Some good water-ing holes: the famed **McSorley's Old Ale House** (15 East 7th St.; 473–8800) in the East Village still looks like a saloon from the last century. The equally woody and warm **White Horse Tavern** (Hudson St. at 11th St.; 243–9260) has the dubious distinction of being the establish-ment where it's said Dylan Thomas drank himself to death. On the sleeker side, the bar at **One Fifth** Restau-rant (8th St. at Fifth Ave.; 260–3434)—modeled on an ocean liner—is a beauty with a lot of late-night action. And for people-watching in the Village, sitting outdoors at the **Riviera Café** (Sheridan Square; 242–8732), weath-er permitting, is a choice location. Uptown, the **Oak Bar** at the Plaza Hotel (Fifth Ave. and 59th St.; 759–3000) is another terrific location, with the bar's huge windows looking out over Central Park. Speaking of views, the one at the bar at the top of the World Trade Towers, the **Hors d'Oeuverie** (1 World Trade Center; 938–1111) is unrivalled—for which you are charged a cover. The bar at the top of the **Beekman Tower** (3 Mitchell Place at 49th St. and First Ave.; 355–7300) is not quite as breath-taking, nor as expensive—a good choice for Midtown. On the swank side, there are the bars at the Carlyle Hotel (Madison Ave. and 76th St.; 744–1600): The **Cafe Car-lyle,** an expensive restaurant with Bobby Short, George Shearing, or Marian McPartland performing; and **Bemel-man's Bar,** frequently featuring Barbara Carroll at the piano. Call first for information on times and covers at each.

After the theater, head to either the legendary **Sar-di's** (234 West 44th St.; 221–8440), with its trademark caricatures of theater greats lining the walls, or the club-by atmosphere of the lobby of the **Algonquin Hotel** (59 West 44th St.; 840–6800), where you'll sit on tapestry-upholstered wing chairs atop Oriental carpets and won-der where Jeeves could be.

When it comes to **theater,** the upper end of the scale is the big name, big Broadway show. Try the TKTS booths (see Midtown section in *Touring the City* chapter) to keep costs down. The quantity of talent in the city is so extensive that Off-Broadway and Off-Off-Broadway (the real avant-garde) shows are of an extremely high caliber. The smaller houses and lack of miking even make this live theater experience more "live" than at the big Broadway houses. Some of the better known and more respected are Joseph Papp's Public Theater (425 La-fayette St.; 598–7150); LaMaMa Experimental Theatre Club (74A East 4th St.; 475–7710); The Provincetown Playhouse (133 MacDougal St.; 944–9300); The Round-about Theatre (100 East 17th St.; 420–1883); Circle in the Square (159 Bleecker St.; 254–6330); Circle Rep (99 Seventh Ave. South; 924–7100); Manhattan Theatre Club, with performances at the City Center (131 West 55th St.; 246–8989); The Mirror Rep (at St. Peter's Church, the Citicorp Center, 54th St. and Lexington Ave.; 223–6440); the long-running *Little Shop of Horrors* (at the Orpheum Theatre, 126 Second Ave.; 239–6262); the even longer-running—27 years!—*The Fantastiks* (at the Sullivan Street Playhouse, 181 Sullivan St.; 674–3838); and certainly some of the most provocative, if not provoking nights at the theater can be spent at the Per-forming Garage (33 Wooster St; 966–3651), home of the Wooster Group whose position at the vanguard of the avant-garde has been set for nearly 20 years.

The lofts of Soho and Tribeca serve up entertain-ment that is hard to put a finger on—it could be a per-formance artist, a poetry reading, rock music, jazz, a concert pianist, you name it. Be prepared for anything—and be prepared to sit on the floor (the early bird might get a pillow). Check the **Kitchen** (512 West 19th St.; 255–5793); the **Franklin Furnace** (112 Franklin St.; 925–4671); P.S. 122 (150 First Ave.; 477–5288); and the list-ings in the *Village Voice.*

If your idea of a night on the town includes some high culture, you've come to the capital. The **dance** line-up includes Balanchine's (now Peter Martins's) New York City Ballet, the star-studded American Ballet Theatre, the Joffrey Ballet, Alvin Ailey, Merce Cunningham, Paul Taylor, The Harlem Dance Studio, and a vast corps of experimental troupes. **Opera** ranges from the world-renowned Metropolitan Opera to the Gilbert and Sullivan operettas at The Light Opera of Manhattan. **Symphony** performances are similarly varied. A concert at the legendary Carnegie Hall—a surprisingly small jewel box—is an event to remember. A short subway ride away, and not to be missed is the Next Wave Festival held at the Brooklyn Academy of Music (30 Lafayette Ave., Brooklyn; 718–636–4100), in late autumn. If you want to know what the world's theaters will be debuting next, the Next Wave Festival is the most important gathering of talent and technique in North America. BAM also features a wide variety of other musical and theatrical treats year-round in a theater whose sight lines and accoustics are among the best in the city. Consult the New York Convention and Visitors Bureau or newspapers and magazines (see selections in this guide's *Introduction*) for information on a selection of performances for you to enjoy.

Index

FODOR'S TRAVEL GUIDES

Here is a complete list of Fodor's Travel Guides, available in current editions; most are also available in a British edition published by Hodder & Stoughton.

U.S. GUIDES

Alaska
American Cities (Great Travel Values)
Arizona including the Grand Canyon
Atlantic City & the New Jersey Shore
Boston
California
Cape Cod & the Islands of Martha's Vineyard & Nantucket
Carolinas & the Georgia Coast
Chesapeake
Chicago
Colorado
Dallas/Fort Worth
Disney World & the Orlando Area (Fun in)
Far West
Florida
Fort Worth (see Dallas)
Galveston (see Houston)
Georgia (see Carolinas)
Grand Canyon (see Arizona)
Greater Miami & the Gold Coast
Hawaii
Hawaii (Great Travel Values)
Houston & Galveston
I-10: California to Florida
I-55: Chicago to New Orleans
I-75: Michigan to Florida
I-80: San Francisco to New York
I-95: Maine to Miami
Jamestown (see Williamsburg)
Las Vegas including Reno & Lake Tahoe (Fun in)
Los Angeles & Nearby Attractions
Martha's Vineyard (see Cape Cod)
Maui (Fun in)
Nantucket (see Cape Cod)
New England
New Jersey (see Atlantic City)
New Mexico
New Orleans
New Orleans (Fun in)
New York City
New York City (Fun in)
New York State
Orlando (see Disney World)
Pacific North Coast
Philadelphia
Reno (see Las Vegas)
Rockies
San Diego & Nearby Attractions
San Francisco (Fun in)
San Francisco plus Marin County & the Wine Country
The South
Texas
U.S.A.
Virgin Islands (U.S. & British)

Virginia
Waikiki (Fun in)
Washington, D.C.
Williamsburg, Jamestown & Yorktown

FOREIGN GUIDES

Acapulco (see Mexico City)
Acapulco (Fun in)
Amsterdam
Australia, New Zealand & the South Pacific
Austria
The Bahamas
The Bahamas (Fun in)
Barbados (Fun in)
Beijing, Guangzhou & Shanghai
Belgium & Luxembourg
Bermuda
Brazil
Britain (Great Travel Values)
Canada
Canada (Great Travel Values)
Canada's Maritime Provinces plus Newfoundland & Labrador
Cancún, Cozumel, Mérida & the Yucatán
Caribbean
Caribbean (Great Travel Values)
Central America
Copenhagen (see Stockholm)
Cozumel (see Cancún)
Eastern Europe
Egypt
Europe
Europe (Budget)
France
France (Great Travel Values)
Germany: East & West
Germany (Great Travel Values)
Great Britain
Greece
Guangzhou (see Beijing)
Helsinki (see Stockholm)
Holland
Hong Kong & Macau
Hungary
India, Nepal & Sri Lanka
Ireland
Israel
Italy
Italy (Great Travel Values)
Jamaica (Fun in)
Japan
Japan (Great Travel Values)
Jordan & the Holy Land
Kenya
Korea
Labrador (see Canada's Maritime Provinces)
Lisbon
Loire Valley
London

London (Fun in)
London (Great Travel Values)
Luxembourg (see Belgium)
Macau (see Hong Kong)
Madrid
Mazatlan (see Mexico's Baja)
Mexico
Mexico (Great Travel Values)
Mexico City & Acapulco
Mexico's Baja & Puerto Vallarta, Mazatlan, Manzanillo, Copper Canyon
Montreal (Fun in)
Munich
Nepal (see India)
New Zealand
Newfoundland (see Canada's Maritime Provinces)
1936 . . . on the Continent
North Africa
Oslo (see Stockholm)
Paris
Paris (Fun in)
People's Republic of China
Portugal
Province of Quebec
Puerto Vallarta (see Mexico's Baja)
Reykjavik (see Stockholm)
Rio (Fun in)
The Riviera (Fun on)
Rome
St. Martin/St. Maarten (Fun in)
Scandinavia
Scotland
Shanghai (see Beijing)
Singapore
South America
South Pacific
Southeast Asia
Soviet Union
Spain
Spain (Great Travel Values)
Sri Lanka (see India)
Stockholm, Copenhagen, Oslo, Helsinki & Reykjavik
Sweden
Switzerland
Sydney
Tokyo
Toronto
Turkey
Vienna
Yucatán (see Cancún)
Yugoslavia

SPECIAL-INTEREST GUIDES

Bed & Breakfast Guide: North America
Royalty Watching
Selected Hotels of Europe
Selected Resorts and Hotels of the U.S.
Ski Resorts of North America
Views to Dine by around the World

AVAILABLE AT YOUR LOCAL BOOKSTORE OR WRITE TO FODOR'S TRAVEL PUBLICATIONS, INC., 201 EAST 50th STREET, NEW YORK, NY 10022.